PIRATES & EMPERORS

PIRATES & EMPERORS

INTERNATIONAL TERRORISM
IN THE REAL WORLD

Noam Chomsky

**BLACK
ROSE
BOOKS**

Montréal · New York

Black Rose Books No. P 113

Canadian Cataloguing in Publication Data

Chomsky, Noam
    Pirates & emperors: international terrorism in the real world

ISBN 0-920057-92-6 (bound). — ISBN 0-920057-93-4 (pbk.).

1. Terrorism. I. Title.

JX5420.C48 1987   303.6'25   C87-090037-4

Cover design: J.W. Stewart

Black Rose Books

3981 boul. St. Laurent
Montréal, Qué. H2W 1Y5
Canada

340 Nagel Dr.
Cheektowaga, N.Y. 14225
USA

Printed and bound in Québec, Canada

Table of Contents

Preface

St. Augustine tells the story of a pirate captured by Alexander the Great. "How dare you molest the sea?" asked Alexander. "How dare you molest the whole world?" the pirate replied. "Because I do it with a little ship only, I am called a thief; you, doing it with a great navy, are called an emperor."

The pirate's answer was "elegant and excellent," St. Augustine relates. It also captures with some accuracy the current relations between the United States and various minor actors on the stage of international terrorism, such as Libya and factions of the PLO. More generally, St. Augustine's tale illuminates the concept of international terrorism in contemporary Western usage, and reaches the heart of the frenzy over selected incidents of terrorism currently being orchestrated, with supreme cynicism, as a cover for Western violence.

The term "terrorism" came into use at the end of the eighteenth century, primarily referring to violent acts of governments designed to ensure popular submission. That concept is plainly of little benefit to the practitioners of state terrorism, who, holding power, are in a position to control the system of thought and expression. The original sense has therefore been abandoned, and the term "terrorism" has come to be applied mainly to "retail terrorism" by individuals or groups. [1] Whereas the term was once applied to emperors who molest their own subjects and the world, it is now restricted to thieves who molest the powerful.

Extricating ourselves from the system of indoctrination, we will use the term "terrorism" to refer to the threat or the use of violence to intimidate or coerce (generally for political ends), whether it is the wholesale terrorism of the emperor or the retail terrorism of the thief.

The pirate's maxim explains the recently-evolved concept of "international terrorism" only in part. It is necessary to add a second feature: an act of terrorism enters the canon only if it is committed by "their side," not ours. Consider, for example, the public relations campaign around "international terrorism" launched in early 1981 by the Reagan Administration. The major text was a book by Claire Sterling,[2] which offered ingenious proof that international terrorism is a "Soviet-inspired" instrument "aimed at the destabilization of Western democratic society." The proof is that the major terrorist actions are confined to the Western democratic states, and are not "directed against the Soviet Union or any of its satellites or client states." This insight much impressed other terrorologists, notably Walter Laqueur, who wrote that Sterling had provided "ample evidence" that terrorism occurs "almost exclusively in democratic or relatively democratic countries."[3]

The Sterling thesis is true, in fact true by definition, given the way in which the term "terrorism" is employed by the emperor and his loyal coterie. Since only acts committed by "their side" count as terrorism, it follows that Sterling is necessarily correct, whatever the facts.

In the real world, the story is different. The major victims of international terrorism[4] in the past several decades have been Cubans, Central Americans, and inhabitants of Lebanon; but none of this counts, by definition. When Israel bombs Palestinian refugee camps, killing many civilians—often without even a pretense of "reprisal"—or sends its troops into Lebanese villages in "counterterror" operations to murder and destroy, or hijacks ships and places hundreds of hostages in prison camps under horrifying conditions, this is not "terrorism." In fact, the rare voices of protest are thunderously condemned by loyal party-liners for their "anti-Semitism" and their "double standards," as demonstrated by their failure to join the chorus of praise for "a country that cares for

10

human life,"[5] whose "high moral purpose"[6] is the object of never-ending awe and acclaim, a country which, according to its American claque, "is held to a higher law, as interpreted for it by journalists" (Walter Goodman).[7]

Neither is it terrorism when paramilitary forces operating from U.S. bases and trained by the CIA bombard Cuban hotels, sink fishing boats and attack Russian ships in Cuban harbours, poison crops and livestock, attempt to assassinate Castro, and so on, in missions that were running almost weekly at their peak.[8] These and innumerable similar actions on the part of the emperor and his clients are not the subject of conferences and learned tomes, nor of anguished commentary and diatribes in the media and journals of opinion.

Standards for the emperor and his court are unique in two closely-related respects. First, their terrorist acts are excluded from the canon, as noted; second, while terrorist attacks against them are regarded with extreme seriousness, even requiring violent "self-defense against future attack," as we will see, comparable or more serious terrorist attacks against others do not merit retaliation or pre-emptive action; if they were to evoke such a response, there would be no end of hysterical outrage in the United States.

Indeed, the significance of such terrorist attacks is so slight that they need barely be reported, surely not remembered.

Suppose, for example, that a seaborne Libyan force were to attack three American ships in the Israeli port of Haifa, sinking one of them and damaging the others, using East German-made missiles. I need not comment on what the reaction would be. Turning to the real world, "on June 5th [1986]," the British press reports, "a seaborne South African force attacked three Russian ships in the southern Angolan harbour of Namibe, sinking one of them," using "Israeli-made Scorpion [Gabriel] missiles."[9]

Had the Soviet Union responded to this terrorist attack like the U.S. would have under similar circumstances— perhaps destroying Johannesburg by firebomb, to judge by the action-response scale of U.S. and Israeli "retaliation"— the U.S. might well have considered a nuclear strike as legitimate "retaliation" against the Communist devil. In the

11

real world, again, the USSR did not respond, and the events were considered so insignificant that they were barely mentioned in the U.S. press.[10]

Suppose Cuba had invaded Venezuela in late 1976 in self-defense against terrorist attack, with the intent of establishing a "New Order" there organised by elements under its control, killing two hundred Americans manning an air defense system, heavily shelling the U.S. embassy in Caracas, and finally occupying the embassy for several days during its conquest of Caracas in violation of a ceasefire agreement.[11] How would the U.S. have responded? The question is academic, since the first sign of a Cuban soldier near Venezuela would probably have evoked a nuclear attack against Havana.

Turning again to the real world, in 1982 Israel attacked Lebanon under the (entirely fabricated) pretext of protecting the Galilee against terrorist attack, with the intent of establishing a "New Order" there organised by elements under its control, killing two hundred Russians manning a (Syrian) air defense system, heavily shelling the Russian embassy in Beirut, and finally occupying the embassy for two days during its conquest of West Beirut in violation of a ceasefire agreement.[12] The facts were casually reported in the U.S., with the context and the crucial background ignored or denied (as we shall see). There was, fortunately, no Soviet response, or we would not be here today to discuss the matter.

In the real world, we assume as a matter of course that the Soviet Union and other official enemies, most of them defenseless, will calmly endure provocations and violence that would elicit a furious reaction, verbal and military, if the emperor and his court were the victims.

The stunning hypocrisy illustrated by these and countless other cases, some of which will be discussed below, is not restricted to the matter of international terrorism. To mention a different case, consider the World War II agreements that allocated control over part of Europe and Asia to the several Allied powers and called for withdrawal at specified times. There was great outrage over indeed outrageous Soviet actions in Eastern Europe modelled closely on what the U.S. had done in the areas assigned to Western control under wartime agreements (Italy, Greece, South Korea, etc.); and over the belated Soviet withdrawal from northern Iran, while the U.S. violated its wartime agreements to withdraw from Portugal, Iceland, Greenland, etc., on the grounds that "military considerations" made such withdrawal "inadvisable," the Joint Chiefs of Staff argued with State Department concurrence.

There was and is no outrage over the fact that West German espionage operations directed against the USSR were placed under the control of Reinhard Gehlen, who had conducted similar operations for the Nazis in Eastern Europe, or that the CIA was sending agents and supplies to armies encouraged by Hitler fighting in Eastern Europe and the Ukraine as late as the early 1950s as part of the "roll-back strategy" made official in NSC-68 (April 1950).[13] Soviet support for armies encouraged by Hitler fighting in the Rockies in 1952 might have elicited a different reaction.

Examples are legion. Perhaps the most notorious is that regularly offered as the ultimate proof that Communists cannot be relied upon to live up to agreements: the 1973 Paris Peace Treaty concerning Vietnam and its aftermath. The truth is that the U.S. announced at once that it would reject every term of the scrap of paper it had been compelled to sign, and proceeded to do so. The media, meanwhile, in a display of servility that goes beyond the norm, accepted the U.S. version of the treaty (violating every essential element of it) as the actual text, so that U.S. violations were "in accord" with the treaty while the Communist reaction to these violations proved their innate treachery. This example is now regularly offered as justification for the U.S. rejection of a negotiated political settlement in Central America, demonstrating the usefulness of a well-run propaganda system.[14]

As noted, "international terrorism" (in the specific Western sense) was placed at the centre of attention by the Reagan Administration as soon as it was installed in 1981.[15] The reasons were not difficult to discern, though they were— and continue to be—inexpressible within the doctrinal system.

The Administration was committed to three related policies, all achieved with considerable success: (1) transfer of resources from the poor to the rich; (2) an enormous increase in the state sector of the economy in the traditional American way, through the Pentagon system, a device used to make the public finance high-technology industry by means of the state-guaranteed market for the production of high-technology waste and thus to contribute to the programme of public subsidy, private profit, called "free enterprise"; and (3) a substantial increase in U.S. intervention, subversion, and international terrorism (in the true sense of the expression). Such policies cannot be presented to the public in the terms in which they are intended. They can be implemented only if the population is properly frightened by monsters against whom they must defend themselves.

The standard device is an appeal to the threat of what the president called "the monolithic and ruthless conspiracy" bent on world conquest—President Kennedy, in this case, when he launched a similar programme[16]—Reagan's "Evil Empire." But confrontation with the Evil Empire can be a dangerous affair. It is much safer to do battle with defenseless enemies designated the Evil Empire's proxies, a choice that conforms to the third plank in the Reagan agenda, pursued for quite independent reasons: to ensure "stability" and "order" in U.S. global domains. The "terrorism" of properly chosen pirates, or of such enemies as Nicaragua or Salvadoran peasants who dare to defend themselves from U.S. terrorist attack, is an easier target—and with an efficiently functioning propaganda system it can be exploited to induce a proper sense of fear and mobilisation in the domestic population.

It is in this context that "international terrorism" replaced human rights as "the Soul of our foreign policy" in the 1980s. Human rights achieved this exalted status as part of the campaign to reverse the notable improvement in the moral and intellectual climate during the 1960s termed the "Vietnam syndrome," and to overcome the dread "crisis of democracy" that erupted in the same context as large elements of the general population organised for political action, threatening the system of elite decision, public ratification, called "democracy" in Western Newspeak.[17]

In what follows, I will be concerned with international terrorism in the real world, focusing on the Mediterranean region. "Mid-East/Mediterranean terrorism" was selected top story of 1985 by editors and broadcasters—primarily American—polled by the Associated Press; the poll was taken before the terrorist attacks at the Rome and Vienna airports in December, which probably would have eliminated remaining doubts.[18] In the early months of 1986, concern over Mid-East/Mediterranean terrorism reached a fever pitch, culminating in the U.S. bombing of Libya in April. The official story is that this courageous punitive action aimed at the leading practitioner of international terrorism achieved its goal. Qaddafi and other such criminals are now cowering in their bunkers, tamed by the noble defender of human rights and dignity.

But despite this grand victory over the forces of darkness, the issue of terrorism emanating from the Islamic world and the proper response for the democracies that defend civilised values remains a leading topic of concern and debate, as illustrated by numerous books, conferences, articles and editorials, and television commentary. Insofar as any large or elite public can be reached, the discussion strictly observes the principles just enunciated: attention is restricted to the terrorism of the thief, not that of the emperor and his clients; on Them, not Us. I will, however, not observe these decencies.

Chapter One is devoted to the conceptual framework in which these and related issues are presented within the reigning doctrinal system. Chapter Two provides a sample—only a sample—of Middle East terrorism in the real world, along with some discussion of the style of apologetics employed to ensure that it proceeds unhampered. In Chapter Three, I will turn to the role played by Libya in the doctrinal system. Chapter Four deals with the role of the United States in the Middle East.

Parts of Chapter One appeared in *Utne Reader* (February-March 1986), *Index on Censorship* (London, July 1986), and *Il Manifesto* (Rome, January 30, 1986). Excerpts from Chapter Two appear in *Race & Class* (London, Summer 1986), and another version will appear in Michael Sprinker, ed., *Negations: Spurious Scholarship and the Palestinian Question* (London: Verso, 1987). Chapter Three is a modified and expanded version of an article that appears under the same title in *Covert Action Information Bulletin*, Summer 1986. Earlier versions of these articles appear in *The New Statesman* (London), *END Papers* (Nottingham), *El Pais* (Madrid), and in Italy, Mexico, Uruguay, and elsewhere. Parts of Chapters Two and Three are also included in my paper "International Terrorism: Image and Reality," delivered at the Frankfurt Conference on International Terrorism in April 1986, to appear in the proceedings, Heinz Dietrich, ed. (London: Zed Press). Chapter Four, which was delivered as a keynote address to the Arab-American University Graduates on November 15, 1986, was published in the *Journal of Palestine Studies*, Vol. 16, No. 3, Spring 1987, pp. 25-42.

Notes

1. "Origins and Fundamental Causes of International Terrorism," U.N. Secretariat, reprinted in M. Cherif Bassiouni, ed., *International Terrorism and Political Crimes* (Charles Thomas, 1975).
2. *The Terror Network* (Holt, Rinehart & Winston, 1981).
3. For references and discussion, see my *Towards a New Cold War* (Pantheon, 1982), p. 47f., and my chapter in Chomsky, Jonathan Steele, and John Gittings, *Superpowers in Collision* (Penguin, 1982, revised edition, 1984). For extensive discussion and documentation on the topic, see Edward S. Herman, *The Real Terror Network* (Black Rose Books, 1985).
4. I exclude here outright aggression, as in the case of the U.S. attack against South Vietnam, then all of Indochina; the Soviet invasion of Afghanistan, the U.S.-backed invasions of Timor and Lebanon by its Indonesian and Israeli clients; etc.
5. *The Washington Post,* June 30, 1985.
6. *Time*, Oct. 11, 1982.
7. *The New York Times*, Feb. 7, 1984.
8. See references of note 3.
9. *The Economist,* June 14; Victoria Brittain, *The Guardian* (London), June 6; Anthony Robinson, *The Financial Times*, June 7, 1986, from Johannesburg. The report was also carried by the BBC World Service. The ship that was sunk may have been a Cuban ship. See also *Israeli Foreign Affairs*, July 1986.
10. There was no mention at all in *The New York Times, The Wall St. Journal, The Christian Science Monitor*, the news weeklies,

nor the other journals listed in the magazine index. *The Washington Post* ran a 120-word item from Moscow on page 17 on June 8, reporting Soviet condemnation of the South African attack.

11.   For background, in October 1976 a Cubana airliner was destroyed in flight by a bomb; seventy-three people were killed, including the entire Cuban Olympic gold-medal fencing team (recall the "Munich massacre," one of the peak moments of Palestinian terrorism). The terrorist action was traced to Orlando Bosch, possibly the leading figure of international terrorism, who had been trained by the CIA along with his close associates in connection with the terrorist war against Cuba and "had close relations with (and has been on the payroll of) the secret police of Chile and Venezuela," who, in turn, "were tutored by the CIA and maintain close relations with it today" (Herman, *The Real Terror Network, op. cit.,* p. 63).

12.   On the Israeli invasion of Lebanon, see Chapter 2 and references cited. The figure of about two hundred Russians killed "Operating in the area of Syrian air defense forces" during the (unprovoked and unexpected) Israeli attack on Syrian forces in Lebanon (which had entered with the agreement of the U.S. and Israel, and were scheduled to complete a six-year stay later that summer, possibly one of the reasons for the timing of the Israeli attack) is given by *Aviation Week & Space Technology,* Dec. 12, 1983. On these events, see Noam Chomsky, *The Fateful Triangle: Israel, the United States, and the Palestinians* (Black Rose Books, 1984).

13.   On the real world, see Gabriel Kolko, *Politics of War* (Random House, 1968), the classic and still unsurpassed account, despite much valuable subsequent scholarship; *Towards a New Cold War, op. cit.*; and my *Turning the Tide: The U.S. and Latin America* (Black Rose Books, rev. ed., 1987), and sources cited; and Melvyn Leffler, "Adherence to Agreements: Yalta and the Experiences of the Early Cold War," *International Security,* Summer 1986. Leffler's conclusion is that "in fact, the Soviet pattern of adherence [to Yalta, Potsdam, and other wartime agreements] was not qualitatively different from the American pattern." It should be noted that in Greece and South Korea in the late 1940s the U.S. organised mass slaughter operations as part of the worldwide programme of destroying the anti-fascist resistance, often in favour of Nazi and Japanese collaborators; see *Turning the Tide*, Chapter 4.4.

14. See *The New Cold War, op. cit.*, Chapter 3, and my introduction to Morris Morley and James Petras, *The Reagan Administration and Nicaragua* (Pamphlet Series, Institute for Media Analysis, New York), forthcoming.

15. The groundwork had already been laid in the United States and in a series of conferences for future terrorologists organised by Israel, which has an obvious interest in this propaganda operation. Commenting on the second Israeli-organised conference on terrorism, held in Washington, Wolf Blitzer observes that the focus on Arab terrorism and the enthusiasm expressed by many notable speakers for Israeli terrorism and aggression (particularly its 1982 invasion of Lebanon) provided "clearly a major boost for Israel's own *Hasbara* campaign in the United States, as recognized by everyone involved" (Wolf Blitzer, *The Jerusalem Post*, June 29, 1984); the word "hasbara" (literally "explanation") is the standard term for Israeli propaganda, expressing the assumption that since Israel's position is so obviously correct on every issue, it is only necessary to "explain," not to produce anything as vulgar as propaganda. For more on the judgements expressed at the conference, see Chapter 3, note 20.

16. Kennedy's programme was limited to the second and third plank of the Reagan agenda; the first, enacted with the support of Congressional Democrats in direct violation of the will of the public, reflects the decline in relative power in the intervening years. It is no longer feasible to pursue "great societies at home and grand designs abroad," in the words of Kennedy adviser Walter Heller, so the former must be abandoned. On public attitudes, see *Turning the Tide, op. cit.*, Chapter 5, and Thomas Ferguson and Joel Rogers, *Atlantic Monthly*, May 1986. On the relation of Reagan's programmes to those of the latter phases of the Carter Administration, which the Reaganites extended, see my *Towards a New Cold War, op. cit.*, Chapter 7, and *Turning the Tide, op. cit.*, Chapters 4 and 5. See also Joshua Cohen and Joel Rogers, *Inequity and Intervention* (South End, 1986).

17. On these matters, see *Towards a New Cold War, op. cit.*, particularly Chapters 1 and 2. The human rights programme, largely a Congressional initiative reflecting the change in public consciousness, was not without significance, despite its exploitation for propaganda purposes and the hypocritical application, which consistently evaded atrocities by client states,

exactly the opposite of the standard charge. For the facts of the matter, see Chomsky and Edward S. Herman, *The Political Economy of Human Rights* (Black Rose Books, 1979), particularly Vol. I: *The Washington Connection and Third World Fascism*.

18. *World Press Review*, Feb. 1986.

CHAPTER ONE
Thought Control:
The Case of the Middle East

From a comparative perspective, the United States is unusual if not unique in its lack of restraints on freedom of expression. It is also unusual in the range and effectiveness of the methods employed to restrain freedom of thought. The two phenomena are related.

Liberal democratic theorists have long observed that in a society where the voice of the people is heard, elite groups must ensure that that voice says the right things. The less the state is able to employ violence to defend the interests of the elite groups that effectively dominate it, the more it becomes necessary to devise techniques for the "manufacture of consent," in the words of Walter Lippmann more than sixty years ago, or the "engineering of consent," the phrase preferred by Edward Bernays, one of the founding fathers of the American public relations industry.[1]

Harold Lasswell wrote in *The Encyclopaedia of the Social Sciences* in 1933 that we must not succumb to "democratic dogmatisms about men being the best judges of their own interests." We must find ways to ensure that they endorse the decisions made by their far-sighted leaders, a lesson learned long before by dominant elites, the rise of the public relations industry being a notable illustration. Where obedience is guaranteed by violence, rulers may lean towards a "behaviourist" conception: it is enough that people obey; what they think does not matter too much. Where the state lacks adequate means of coercion, it is important to control what people think as well.

The attitude is common among intellectuals across the political spectrum, and is retained when they shift across this spectrum as circumstances dictate. A version was expressed by the highly respected moralist and political commentator Reinhold Niebuhr when he wrote in 1932—then from a Christian left perspective—that given "the stupidity of the average man," it is the responsibility of "cool observers" to provide the "necessary illusion" so that faith is instilled in the minds of the less endowed.[2]

The doctrine is also familiar in its Leninist version, and in American social science and liberal commentary generally. Consider the bombing of Libya in April 1986. We read without surprise that it was a public relations success in the United States. It "is playing well in Peoria" and its "positive political impact" should "strengthen President Reagan's hand in dealing with Congress on issues like the military budget and aid to Nicaraguan 'contras'." "This sort of public education campaign is the essence of statecraft," according to Dr. Everett Ladd, a leading academic public opinion specialist. He added that a president "must be engaged in the engineering of democratic consent," using the inspired Orwellism common in public relations and academic circles to refer to the methods for undermining meaningful democratic participation in shaping public policy.[3]

The problem of "engineering democratic consent" arises in a particularly sharp form when state policy is indefensible, and becomes serious to the extent that the issues are serious. There is no doubt about the gravity of Middle East issues, particularly the Arab-Israeli conflict, which is commonly—and plausibly—judged the "tinder box" most likely to set off nuclear war as regional conflict engages the superpowers, something that has come quite close in the past and will again. Furthermore, U.S. policy has contributed materially to maintaining the state of military confrontation and is based on implicit racist assumptions that would not be tolerated if stated openly. There is also a marked divergence

22

between popular attitudes, generally supportive of a Palestinian state when the question is raised in polls, and state policy, which explicitly bars this option. The divergence is of little moment, however, as long as the politically active and articulate elements of the population maintain proper discipline. To assure this outcome, it is necessary to conduct what American historians called "historical engineering" when they lent their talents to the Wilson Administration during World War I in one of the early exercises in organised "manufacture of consent." There is a variety of ways in which this result is achieved.

One method is to devise a form of Newspeak in which crucial terms have a technical sense, divorced from their ordinary meanings. Consider, for example, the term "peace process." In its technical sense, as used in the mass media and scholarship generally in the United States, it refers to peace proposals advanced by the U.S. government. It is thus true by definition that the United States is committed to peace. Right-thinking people hope that Jordan will join the peace process; that is, will accept U.S. dictates. The big question is whether the PLO will agree to join the peace process, or will be granted admission to this august ceremony.

The headline of a review of the "peace process" by Bernard Gwertzman in *The New York Times* reads: "Are the Palestinians Ready to Seek Peace?"[4] In the normal sense of the term "peace," the answer is, of course, "yes." Everyone seeks peace, on their own terms; Hitler, for example, surely sought peace in 1939, on his terms. But in the system of thought control, the question means something else: are the Palestinians ready to accept U.S. terms for peace? These terms happen to deny them the right of national self-determination, but unwillingness to accept this consequence demonstrates that the Palestinians do not seek peace as defined in conventional Newspeak.

Note that it is unnecessary for Gwertzman to ask whether the United States or Israel is "ready to seek peace." For the U.S., this is true by definition, and the conventions of what is called "responsible journalism" (another Orwellism) entail that the same must be true for a well-behaved client state.

Gwertzman asserts further that the PLO has always rejected "any talk of negotiated peace with Israel." That is false, but it is true in the world of "necessary illusion" constructed by the Newspaper of Record, which, along with other responsible journals, has either suppressed the relevant facts or relegated them to Orwell's useful memory hole.

Of course, there are Arab peace proposals, including PLO proposals, but these are not part of the "peace process." Thus, in a review of "Two Decades of Seeking Peace in the Middle East," *The Times* Jerusalem correspondent Thomas Friedman excludes the major Arab (including PLO) peace proposals; no Israeli proposals are listed, because no serious ones have been advanced, a fact not discussed for obvious reasons.[5]

What is the character of the official "peace process" and the Arab proposals excluded from it? Before answering this question, we must clarify another Newspeak term: "rejectionism." In its Orwellian usage, this term refers to the position of Arabs who deny the right of national self-determination to Israeli Jews, or who refuse to accept Israel's "right to exist." This novel and ingenious concept is designed to bar Palestinians from the "peace process" by demonstrating the "extremism" of those who refuse to accept what they see as the robbery of their homeland, and who reject the traditional view—the view adopted by the reigning ideological system in the U.S. and the prevailing international practice with regard to every state apart from Israel—that while states are recognised within the international order, their "right to exist" is not.

There are elements in the Arab world to which the term "rejectionist" applies: Libya, the minority Rejection Front of the PLO, and others. But it should not escape notice that in official Newspeak, the term is used in a strictly racist sense.

Abandoning racist assumptions, we observe that there are two groups that claim the right of national self-determination in the former Palestine: the indigenous population, who were always a large majority before the establishment of the state of Israel, and the Jewish settlers who largely displaced them, at times with a considerable amount of violence.

24

Presumably, the indigenous population have rights comparable to those of the Jewish immigrants (some might argue that this does not go far enough, but I put that issue to the side). If so, then the term "rejectionism" should be used to refer to denial of the right of national self-determination to one or the other of the competing national groups. But the term cannot be used in its nonracist sense within the U.S. doctrinal system, or it will be seen at once that the U.S. and Israel lead the rejectionist camp, an intolerable insight in the real world.

With these clarifications, we can turn to the question: what is the "peace process"?

The official "peace process" is explicitly rejectionist, including the position of the United States and both major political groups in Israel. Their rejectionism is, in fact, so extreme that the Palestinians are not even to be permitted to select their own representatives in eventual negotiations about their fate—just as they are denied municipal elections and other democratic forms under the Israeli military occupation.

Is there a nonrejectionist peace proposal (in the nonracist sense of the term) on the agenda? In the U.S. doctrinal system, the answer is, of course, "no," by definition. But in the real world, matters are different. The basic terms of this proposal are familiar, reflecting a broad international consensus: they include a Palestinian state on the West Bank and Gaza Strip alongside Israel and the principle that "it is essential to ensure the security and sovereignty of all states of the region including those of Israel."

The quoted words are those of Leonid Brezhnev expressing the standard Soviet position in an address to the Soviet Communist Party Congress of February 1981. Brezhnev's speech was excerpted in *The New York Times*, however, with such crucial segments omitted; while cuts in a Reagan post-summit statement in *Pravda* evoked much righteous indignation. In April 1981, Brezhnev's statement was unanimously endorsed by the PLO, but this was not reported in *The Times*. Official doctrine holds that the Soviet Union is interested only in causing trouble and blocking peace, and thus supports

Arab rejectionism and extremism. The media dutifully fulfill their assigned role.

One might cite other examples. In October 1977, a joint Carter-Brezhnev statement called for the "termination of the state of war and establishment of normal peaceful relations" between Israel and its neighbours. This was endorsed by the PLO, and withdrawn by Carter after a furious reaction by Israel and its American lobby. In January 1976, Jordan, Syria, and Egypt submitted a proposal for a two-state settlement to the U.N. Security Council in accordance with international consensus. This proposal was endorsed by the PLO; according to Israel's President Chaim Herzog (then ambassador to the U.N.), it was "prepared" by the PLO. It was vetoed by the United States.[6]

Much of this has been eliminated from history, in journalism and scholarship. The 1976 Arab initiative is not even mentioned in the unusually careful review by Seth Tillman in his book *The United States and the Middle East* (Indiana, 1982). It is mentioned by Steven Spiegel in *The Other Arab-Israeli Conflict* (Chicago, 1985, p. 306), a much-praised work of scholarship, along with some remarkable commentary. Spiegel writes that the U.S. "vetoed the pro-Palestinian resolution" so as "to demonstrate that the United States was willing to hear Palestinian aspirations but would not accede to demands that threatened Israel."

The commitment to U.S.-Israeli rejectionism could not be clearer, and is accepted as quite proper in the United States, along with the principle that demands that threaten the Palestinians are entirely legitimate, indeed praiseworthy: the terms of the official "peace process," for example. In public discussion, it is a matter of doctrine that the Arab states and the PLO have never veered from their absolute refusal to come to terms with Israel, apart from Sadat after his trip to Jerusalem in 1977. Facts need be no embarrassment, or even mild annoyance, to a well-functioning system of "historical engineering."

Israel's reaction to the 1976 peace proposal of the PLO and the "confrontation states" was to bomb Lebanon (without a pretense of "retaliation," except against the U.N. Security Council), killing more than fifty people, and to announce that Israel would not deal with any Palestinians on any political issue. This was the dovish Labour government headed by Yitzhak Rabin, who, in his memoirs, identifies two forms of "extremism": that of the Begin government, and the proposal of "the Palestinian extremists (basically the PLO)" "to create a sovereign Palestinian state in the West Bank and the Gaza Strip." Only the Labour Party style of rejectionism departs from "extremism," a position shared by American commentators.[7]

We note incidentally another pair of Newspeak concepts: "extremist" and "moderate," the latter referring to those who accept the position of the United States, the former to those who do not. The American position is thus by definition moderate, as is that of the Israeli Labour coalition (generally), since its rhetoric tends to approximate that of the United States. Rabin thus conforms to approved practice in his use of the terms "moderate" and "extremist."

Similarly, in a suitably anguished review of "extremism" and its ascendance, Thomas Friedman includes under this rubric those who advocate a nonracist settlement in accord with the international consensus, while the Western leaders of the rejectionist camp, who are also far in the lead in terrorist operations, are the "moderates"; by definition, one might add. Friedman writes that "extremists have always been much better at exploiting the media." And he is quite right: Israel and the U.S. have shown unparalleled mastery of this art, as his own articles and news reports indicate— leading some to wonder whether he should not be called "Israel's *Times* correspondent."[8] His convenient version of history and the conceptual framework of his reporting, as just illustrated, provide a few of the many examples of the success of extremists in "exploiting the media"—now using the term in its non-Orwellian sense.

In adopting this conceptual framework, which is designed to exclude any possible comprehension of the facts and issues, *The Times* follows the practice of such Israeli models as Rabin, who achieve the status of "moderates" by virtue of their general conformity to U.S. government demands. It is, correspondingly, entirely natural that when Friedman reviews "Two Decades of Seeking Peace in the Mideast," major proposals rejected by the U.S. and Israel are omitted, as inappropriate for the historical record.

Meanwhile, Israeli leaders are praised by *The Times* editors for their "healthy pragmatism," while the PLO is denounced for standing in the way of peace.[9]

It is, incidentally, a staple of the ideological system that the media are highly critical of Israel and the U.S. and are far too forthcoming in their tolerance of Arab extremists. The fact that such statements can even be made without evoking ridicule is one sign of the extraordinary success of the system of indoctrination.

Returning to the "extremists," in April-May 1984, Yasser Arafat issued a series of statements calling for negotiations leading to mutual recognition. The U.S. national press refused to publish the facts; *The Times* even banned letters referring to them, while continuing to denounce the "extremist" Arafat for blocking a peaceful settlement.[10]

These and many other examples illustrate that there are nonrejectionist proposals that are widely supported; in fact, they are supported with some variations by most of Europe, the USSR, the nonaligned states, the major Arab states and PLO mainstream, and a majority of American public opinion (to judge by the few existing polls). But they are not part of the peace process because the United States opposes them. The examples cited are thus excluded from the *Times* review of "Two Decades of Seeking Peace," and from the journalistic and even scholarly literature generally.

There are other incidents that do not qualify as part of the peace process. Thus, the *Times* review does not mention Anwar Sadat's offer of a full peace treaty on the internationally recognised borders—in accord with official U.S. rhetoric at the time—in February 1971, which was rejected by Israel with U.S. backing.

Note that this proposal was rejectionist in that it offered nothing to the Palestinians. In his memoirs, Henry Kissinger explains his policy at that time: "Until some Arab state showed a willingness to separate from the Soviets, or the Soviets were prepared to dissociate from the maximum Arab program, we had no reason to modify our policy" of "stale-mate." The USSR was extremist, in the technical sense, supporting what happened to be official (though not operative) U.S. policy.

Kissinger was right, of course, to point out that such Arab states as Saudi Arabia refused to "separate from the Soviets." He did not observe, however—and is apparently unaware—that this would have been a logical impossibility, since Saudi Arabia did not even have diplomatic relations with the USSR, and never had.

The impressive discipline of the media and scholarship is revealed by the fact that these astonishing statements escape comment, just as no responsible commentator would express the truth that Kissinger's blissful ignorance and insistence on military confrontation was the primary cause of the 1973 war.[11]

Sadat's proposal has been expunged from the historical record. The official story is that Sadat was a typical Arab thug, interested only in killing Jews, though he saw the error of his ways after his failed attempt to destroy Israel in 1973 and, under the kindly tutelage of Kissinger and Carter, became a man of peace. Thus, in its two-page obituary after Sadat's assassination, *The Times* not only suppresses the actual facts but explicitly denies them, stating that until his 1977 trip to Jerusalem Sadat was unwilling "to accept Israel's existence as a sovereign state."[12] *Newsweek* refused even to print a letter correcting outright falsehoods on this matter by their columnist George Will, though the research department privately conceded the facts. The practice is standard.

The terms "terrorism" and "retaliation" also have a special sense in U.S. Newspeak. "Terrorism" refers to terrorist acts by various pirates, particularly Arabs. Terrorist acts by the emperor and his clients are termed "retaliation," or perhaps "legitimate pre-emptive strikes to avert terrorism" quite independently of the facts, as will be discussed in the following chapters.

The term "hostage"—like "terrorism," "moderate," "democratic," and other terms of political discourse—also has a technical Orwellian sense within the reigning doctrinal system. In the dictionary sense of the words, the people of Nicaragua are now being held hostage in a major terrorist operation directed from the centres of international terrorism in Washington and Miami. The purpose of this campaign of international terrorism is to induce changes in the behaviour of the Nicaraguan government: crucially, an end to programmes that direct resources to the poor majority and a return to "moderate" and "democratic" policies that favour U.S. business interests and their local associates.

A very powerful case can be made that this is the central reason for the U.S.-run terrorist war against Nicaragua, a case that is not rejected but is rather not open for discussion within the U.S. system of thought control.[13] This is a particularly sadistic exercise in terrorism, not only because of the scale and the evident purpose, but also because of the means employed, which go well beyond the usual practice of the retail terrorists whose exploits arouse such horror in civilised circles: Leon Klinghoffer and Natasha Simpson were murdered by terrorists, but not first subjected to brutal torture, mutilation, rape, and the other standard practices of U.S.-trained and U.S.-supported terrorists, as the record— generally ignored in the U.S.—makes abundantly clear.

U.S. policy is to ensure that the terrorist attacks continue until the government yields or is overthrown, while the emperor's minions preach soothing words about "democracy" and "human rights."

But in Orwellian usage, the terms "terrorism" and "hostage" are restricted to a certain class of terrorist acts: not the wholesale terrorism of the emperor, but rather the retail terrorism of the pirate, directed against those who regard terrorism and the holding of hostages on a grand scale as their prerogative. In the Middle East, Israeli piracy, hostage-taking, and terrorist attacks on defenseless villages do not fall under the concept of terrorism, as properly construed within the doctrinal system.

The record of deceit concerning terrorism, to which I will turn in the chapters that follow, is so extensive that it can only be sampled here. It is highly instructive with regard to the functioning of Western propaganda and the nature of Western culture.

The relevant point here is that a proper history and appropriate form of Newspeak have been contrived in which terrorism is the province of the Palestinians, while the Israelis carry out "retaliation," or sometimes legitimate "pre-emption," occasionally reacting with regrettable harshness, as any state would do under such trying circumstances.

The doctrinal system is designed to ensure that these conclusions are true by definition, regardless of the facts, which are either not reported or reported in such a manner as to conform to doctrinal necessities, or—occasionally—reported honestly but then dismissed to the memory hole.

Israel is a loyal and very useful client state, a "strategic asset" in the Middle East willing to support near-genocide in Guatemala when the U.S. Administration is prevented by Congress from joining as fully as it would have liked in this necessary exercise. It therefore becomes true, irrespective of the facts, that Israel is dedicated to the highest moral values and "purity of arms," while the Palestinians are the very epitome of extremism, terrorism, and barbarity. The suggestion that there might be a certain symmetry, both in rights and in terrorist practice, is dismissed with outrage in the mainstream—or it would be, if the words could be heard—as barely disguised anti-Semitism. A rational assessment, giving an accurate portrayal and analysis of the scale and purposes of the terrorism of the emperor and the pirate, is excluded *a priori*, and would indeed be barely comprehensible, so remote would it be from received orthodoxies.

Israel's services to the U.S. as a "strategic asset" in the Middle East and elsewhere help explain the dedication of the United States, since Kissinger's takeover of Middle-East policy-making in the early 1970s, to maintaining the military confrontation and Kissingerian "stalemate."[14] If the U.S. were to permit a peaceful settlement in accord with the international consensus, Israel would gradually be incorporated into the region and the U.S. would lose the services of a valuable mercenary state, militarily competent and technologically advanced—a pariah state, utterly dependent upon the United States for its economic and military survival and hence dependable, available for service where needed.

Elements of the "Israeli lobby" also have a stake in maintaining the military confrontation, as Israeli journalist Danny Rubinstein of the Labour Party journal *Davar* discovered on a visit to the United States in 1983.[15] In meetings with representatives of the major Jewish organisations (B'nai Brith, the Anti-Defamation League, the World Jewish Congress, Hadassah, rabbis of all denominations, etc.), Rubinstein discovered that his presentations on the current situation in Israel aroused considerable hostility because he stressed the fact that Israel did not face military danger so much as "political, social, and moral destruction" because of the takeover of the occupied territories. "I am not interested," one functionary told him. "I can't do anything with such an argument." The point, Rubinstein discovered in many such interchanges, is that

> according to most of the people in the Jewish establishment the important thing is to stress again and again the external dangers that face Israel... the Jewish establishment in America needs Israel only as a victim of a cruel Arab attack. For such an Israel one can get support, donors, and money. How can one raise money for fighting a demographic danger? Who will give even a single dollar to fight what I call "the danger of annexation"?... Everybody knows the official tally of the contributions collected by the United Jewish Appeal in America, where the name of Israel is used and about half of the sum does not go to Israel but to the Jewish institutions in America. Is there a greater cynicism?

Rubinstein goes on to observe that the Appeal,

> which is managed as a tough and efficient business, has a common language with the hawkish positions in Israel. On the other hand, the attempt to communicate with Arabs, the striving for mutual recognition with the Palestinians, the moderate, dovish positions all work against the business of collecting contributions. They not only reduce the sum of money that is transferred to Israel. More to the point, they reduce the amount of money that is available for financing the activities of the Jewish communities.

Observers of the regular activities of the Israeli lobby thought police, keen to detect the slightest hint of a suggestion about reconciliation and a meaningful political settlement and to demolish this heresy with furious articles and letters to the press, circulation of fabricated defamatory material concerning the heretics, etc., will know just what Rubinstein was encountering.

Rubinstein's comments bring to our attention yet another Orwellism: the term "supporters of Israel," used conventionally to refer to those who are not troubled by "the political, social, and moral destruction" of Israel (and, in the longer term, probably its physical destruction as well), and indeed contribute to these consequences by the "blindly chauvinistic and narrow-minded" support they offer to Israel's "posture of calloused intransigence," as Israeli doves have often warned. [16]

In the same connection, we may observe the interesting way in which the term "Zionism" is currently defined — tacitly, of course — by those who take on the role of guardians of doctrinal purity. My own views, for example, are regularly condemned as "militant anti-Zionism" by people who are well aware of these views, repeatedly and clearly expressed: that Israel within its internationally recognised borders should be accorded the rights of any state in the international system, no more, no less, and that discriminatory institutional structures that in law and in practice assign a special status to one category of citizens (Jews, Whites, Christians, etc.), granting them rights denied others, should be dismantled. I will not enter here into the question of what should propoerly be called "Zionism," but merely note what follows from designation of these views as "militant anti-Zionism": Zionism is the doctrine that Israel must be accorded rights beyond those of any other state; it must maintain control of occupied territories, thus barring any meaningful form of self-determination for Palestinians; and it must remain a state based on the principle of discrimination against non-Jewish citizens. It is intriguing, in particular, to observe that "supporters of Israel" insist on the validity of the notorious U.N. resolution on Zionism and racism.

It should be noted that these questions are not abstract and theoretical. The problem of discrimination is severe in Israel. For example, more than ninety percent of the land is placed, by law, under the control of an organisation devoted to the interests of "persons of Jewish religion, race, or origin," so that non-Jewish citizens are effectively excluded. The commitment to discriminatory practice is so profound that the issue cannot even be addressed in parliament, where new laws bar presentation of any bill that "negates the existence of the State of Israel as the state of the Jewish people," not of its citizens. The legislation thus renders illegal any parliamentary challenge to the fundamentally discriminatory character of the state and effectively bars political parties committed to the standard democratic principle that a state is the state of its citizens.[17]

It is remarkable that the Israeli press and most educated opinion appear to have perceived nothing strange about the fact that this legislation was coupled with an "anti-racism" bill (the four opposing votes, in fact, were against this aspect of the measure). *The Jerusalem Post* headline reads: "Knesset forbids racist and anti-Zionist bills"—without irony, the term "Zionist" being interpreted as in the new legislation. U.S. readers of *The Jerusalem Post* apparently also found nothing noteworthy in this conjunction, just as they have never had any difficulty reconciling the fundamentally anti-democratic character of their version of Zionism with enthusiastic acclaim for the democratic character of the state in which it is realised.

No less remarkable are the ingenious uses of the concept "anti-Semitism"—for example, to refer to those who exhibit "the anti- imperialism of fools" (a variety of anti-Semitism) by objecting to Israel's role in the Third World in the service of the U.S.—in Guatemala, for example—or to Palestinians who refuse to understand that their problem can be overcome by "resettlement and some repatriation." If the remnants of the village of Doueimah, where hundreds were slaughtered by the Israeli army in a land-clearing operation in 1948, or residents of the Soweto-like Gaza Strip object, it proves that they are inspired by "anti-Semitism."[18] One would have to descend to the lower depths of the annals of Stalinism to find anything similar, but comparable examples in educated discourse in the United States with regard to Israel are not at all rare, and pass unnoticed there, though Israeli doves have not failed to perceive, and to condemn, the Stalinist style.

The central device of the system of "brainwashing under freedom," developed in a most impressive fashion in the United States, is to encourage debate over policy issues but within a framework of presuppositions that incorporate the basic doctrines of the party line. The more vigorous the debate, the more effectively these presuppositions are instilled, while the participants and onlookers are overcome with awe and self-adulation for their courage and for the remarkable freedoms upheld in their society.

Thus in the case of the Vietnam war, the ideological institutions permitted a debate between "hawks" and "doves." In fact, the debate was not only permitted, but even encouraged, by 1968, when substantial sectors of American business had turned against the war as too costly and harmful to their interests. The hawks held that with firmness and dedication the United States could succeed in its "defense of South Vietnam against Communist aggression." The doves countered by questioning the feasibility of this noble effort, or deplored the excessive use of force and violence in pursuing it. Or they bewailed the "errors" and "misunderstandings" that misled us in our "excess of righteousness and disinterested benevolence" (Harvard historian John King Fairbank, the dean of U.S. Asian studies and a noted academic dove) and "blundering efforts to do good" (Anthony Lewis, probably the leading media dove). Or sometimes, at the outer reaches of the doctrinal system, they asked whether indeed North Vietnam and the Viet Cong were guilty of aggression; perhaps, they suggested, the charge is exaggerated.

The central and most obvious fact about the war, plainly enough, was that the U.S. was not "defending" South Vietnam. It was attacking South Vietnam, surely from 1962, when President Kennedy dispatched the U.S. air force to take part in the large-scale bombing and defoliation designed to help drive millions of people into concentration camps. There they could be "protected" from the South Vietnamese guerrillas they were willingly supporting (as the U.S. government privately conceded), after the U.S. had undermined any possibility of political settlement and had installed a

35

murderous client regime which, by then, had killed perhaps a hundred thousand South Vietnamese. Throughout the war, the major U.S. assault was against South Vietnam, and it did succeed, by the late 1960s, in destroying the South Vietnamese resistance while spreading the war to the rest of Indochina.

When the USSR attacks Afghanistan, we perceive it as aggression; but when the U.S. attacks South Vietnam, it is "defense"—defense against "internal aggression," as Adlai Stevenson proclaimed at the United Nations in 1964, when his government was secretly planning to expand the aggression in intensity and scope. That the U.S. was engaged in an attack against South Vietnam was not denied by the propaganda system; rather, the thought could not be expressed or even imagined. One will find no hint of such an event as "the U.S. attack against South Vietnam" in mainstream media or scholarship, or even in most peace movement publications. [19]

There is no more striking example of the extraordinary power of the American system of thought control than the debate that took place over North Vietnamese aggression and whether the U.S. had the right under international law to combat it in "collective self-defense against armed attack." Learned tomes were written advocating the opposing positions, and in less exalted terms, the debate was pursued in the public arena opened by the peace movement.

The debate was a magnificent reflection of the system of thought control, as well as a contribution to it, since as long as debate is focused on the question of whether the Vietnamese are guilty of aggression in Vietnam, there can be no discussion of whether the U.S. aggression against South Vietnam was indeed what it plainly was.

As one who took part in this debate, with complete consciousness of what was happening, I can only report the recognition that opponents of state violence were trapped, enmeshed in a propaganda system of awesome effectiveness. It was necessary for critics of the U.S. war in Vietnam to become experts in the intricacies of Indochinese affairs; largely an irrelevance, since the issue—always avoided—was U.S. affairs, just as we need not become specialists in Afghanistan to oppose Soviet aggression there. It was necessary, throughout, to enter the arena of debate on the terms set by the state and the elite opinion that loyally serves it, however one might understand that by doing so, one is making a further contribution to the system of indoctrination. The alternative is to tell the truth, which would be equivalent to speaking in some foreign tongue.

Much the same is true of the current debate over Central America. The U.S. terrorist war in El Salvador is not a topic for discussion among respectable people; it does not exist. The U.S. effort to "contain" Nicaragua is a permissible subject of debate, but within narrow limits.

We may ask whether it is right to use force to "excise the cancer" and prevent the Sandinistas from exporting their "revolution without borders" (a fanciful construction of the propaganda system, known to be a fabrication by the journalists and other commentators who obediently parrot the government charge). But we may not discuss the fact that "the cancer" that must be excised is "the threat of a good example," which might spread "contagion" through the region and beyond.

Thus in the first three months of 1986, when debate was intensifying over the impending Congressional votes on aid to the U.S. proxy army (as its most enthusiastic supporters privately describe it) attacking Nicaragua from its Honduran and Costa Rican bases, the U.S. national press (*The New York Times* and *The Washington Post*) ran no fewer than eighty-five opinion pieces by columnists and invited contributors on U.S. policy towards Nicaragua. All eighty-five were critical of the Sandinistas, ranging from bitterly critical (the vast majority) to moderately critical.

This is what is called "public debate" in the United States. The unquestioned fact that the Sandinista government had carried out successful, in fact quite remarkable social reforms during the early years, before the U.S. war aborted these efforts, was close to unmentionable; in eighty-five columns, there were two phrases referring to the fact that there had been such social reforms, and the fact—hardly a great secret—that this is the basic reason for the U.S. attack was, of course, entirely unmentionable, indeed unthinkable.

Alleged "apologists" for the Sandinistas were harshly denounced (anonymously, to ensure that they would have no opportunity to respond, minimal as that possibility would be in any event), but none of these criminals was permitted to express their views.

It is hardly imaginable that the American national press would permit expression of the conclusion of the charitable development agency Oxfam. Nicaragua was "exceptional" among the seventy-six developing countries in which Oxfam worked, it said, in the commitment of the political leadership "to improving the condition of the people and encouraging their active participation in the development process." Among the four Central American countries in which Oxfam worked, "only in Nicaragua has a substantial effort been made to address inequities in land ownership and to extend health, educational, and agricultural services to poor peasant families," though the *contra* war has terminated these threats and caused Oxfam to shift its efforts from development projects to war relief.

It is inconceivable that the national press in the U.S. would permit discussion of the fact that the dedicated U.S. effort to excise this "cancer" falls strictly within its historical vocation, just as respectable scholarship must pretend not to perceive such unacceptable truths. Debate may proceed over the proper method for combatting this vicious outpost of the Evil Empire, but may not go beyond these boundaries in a national forum. [20]

As in the case of Indochina, we see here—in the permitted range of expressible opinion—the remarkable success of "brainwashing under freedom," and, as any honest person should easily understand, the reflection of a totalitarian mentality under conditions where resources of state violence are not available to ensure strict obedience. [21]

In a dictatorship or military-run "democracy," the party line is clear, overt, and explicit, either announced by the Ministry of Truth or made apparent in other ways. And it must be publicly obeyed; the cost of disobedience ranges from prison and exile under terrible conditions, as in the USSR and its East European satellites, to hideous torture, rape, mutilation, and mass slaughter, as in a typical U.S.

dependency such as El Salvador. In a free society, these devices are not available and more subtle means are used to ensure thought control. The party line is not enunciated, but is rather presupposed. Those who do not accept it are not imprisoned or deposited in ditches after torture and mutilation, but the population is nonetheless protected from their heresies.

Within the mainstream, it is barely possible even to understand their words on the rare occasions when such exotic discourse can be heard. In the mediaeval period, when standards of integrity and intellectual honesty were far higher, it was considered necessary to take heresy seriously, to understand it and combat it by rational argument. Today, it suffices to point to it. A whole battery of concepts have been concocted—such as "moral equivalence," or "Marxist," or "radical"—to identify heresy, and thus to dismiss it without further argument or comment.

These dangerous doctrines even become "new orthodoxies"[22] to be combatted (or, more accurately, identified and dismissed, since serious intellectual engagement is considered inappropriate) by the embattled minority who dominate public expression to something close to—but, unfortunately, in their eyes, not quite—totality. But for the most part heresy is simply ignored, while debate rages over narrow and generally marginal issues among those who accept the Doctrines of the Faith, typically without thought or awareness.

Very much the same is true when we turn to our present topic, the Middle East. We may debate whether the Palestinians should be allowed to enter "the peace process," but we must not be permitted to understand that the U.S. and Israel lead the rejectionist camp and have consistently blocked any authentic "peace process," often with substantial violence.

With regard to terrorism, the bounds of permissible debate are clearly indicated by Shaul Bakhash, professor of history at George Mason University, who explains that we should refrain from the "oversimplification" that avoids any attempt "to examine the social and ideological roots of current Middle Eastern and Islamic radicalism," which raises "intractable but nevertheless real problems"; we should seek to understand what leads the terrorists to pursue their evil ways.[23]

The debate over terrorism, then, is neatly demarcated; at one extreme, we have those who see it as simply a conspiracy by the Evil Empire and its agents. At the other extreme, we find those more balanced and astute thinkers who avoid this "oversimplification" and also seek the domestic roots of Arab and Islamic terror. The idea that there may be other sources of terrorism in the Middle East—that the emperor and his clients may also have a hand in the drama—is excluded *a priori*; it is not denied, but is unthinkable, a true triumph of a doctrinal system that far surpasses the achievements of totalitarian states in protecting the public against improper thoughts.

Notice that throughout, it is the contributions of the "moderates," the liberal doves, that ensure the proper functioning of the indoctrination system, by setting firmly the bounds of thinkable thought.

In his *Journal*, Henry David Thoreau, who explained elsewhere that he wasted no time reading newspapers, wrote that

> There is no need of a law to check the license of the press. It is law enough, and more than enough, to itself. Virtually, the community have come together and agreed what things shall be uttered, have agreed on a platform and to excommunicate him who departs from it, and not one in a thousand dares utter anything else.

Thoreau's statement is not quite accurate, John Dolan observes: it "is not that people will lack the courage to express thoughts outside the permitted range: it is, rather, that they will lack the capacity to think such thoughts."[24] That is the essential point, the driving motive of the "engineers of democratic consent."

In *The New York Times*, Walter Reich of the Woodrow Wilson International Center, referring to the *Achille Lauro* hijacking, demands that strict standards of justice be applied to people who have "committed terrorist murder," both the agents and planners of these acts:

> To mete out lesser punishment on the grounds that a terrorist believes himself to be a deprived, aggrieved freedom fighter undermines the ground on which justice stands by accepting terrorists' arguments that only their concepts of justice and rights, and their sufferings, are valid.... The Palestinians—and any of the many groups using terrorism to satisfy grievances—should scuttle terror and find other ways, inevitably involving compromise, to achieve their goals. And the Western democracies must reject the argument that any excuse—even one involving a background of deprivation—can "attenuate" responsibility for terrorism against innocents.

Noble words, and ones which might even be taken seriously if the stern injunction to carry out harsh punitive action were applied to oneself, to the emperor and his clients; if not, these strictures have all the merit of no less high-minded phrases produced by the World Peace Council and other Communist-front organisations with regard to the atrocities of the Afghan resistance.

Mark Heller, deputy director of the Jaffee Center for Strategic Studies at Tel Aviv University, explains that "State-sponsored terrorism is low-intensity warfare, and its victims, including the United States, are therefore entitled to fight back with every means at their disposal": Salvadorans, Nicaraguans, Palestinians, Lebanese, and innumerable other victims of the emperor and his clients throughout a good part of the world.[25]

But these consequences neither Reich nor Heller could comprehend, nor could most of their readers, nor would they be expressible in *The New York Times*. In fact, were anyone to draw the logical consequences of Reich's and Heller's dicta and to express them clearly, they might be subject to prosecution for inciting terrorist violence against the political leaders of the United States and its allies.

The most sceptical voices in the U.S. agree that "Colonel Qaddafi's open support of terrorism is a blatant evil," and that "there is no reason to let murders go unpunished if you

41

know their author [*sic*]. Nor can it be a decisive factor that retaliation will kill some innocent civilians, or murderous states would never fear retribution."[26]

This principle entitles large numbers of people around the world to assassinate President Reagan and to bomb Washington even if this "retaliation will kill some innocent civilians." It is unlikely that more than a tiny fraction of educated Americans could comprehend these simple truths, and they are hardly likely to be expressible within the doctrinal system. As long as this remains true—in the cases I have mentioned and many others—we delude ourselves if we believe that we participate in a democratic polity, except in the Orwellian sense of educated discourse.

There is agonised debate in the media over whether it is proper to permit the pirates and thieves to express their demands and perceptions; NBC, for example, was bitterly condemned for running an interview with the man accused of planning the *Achille Lauro* hijacking, thus serving the interests of terrorists by allowing them free expression without rebuttal—a shameful departure from the uniformity demanded in a properly functioning free society.

Should the media permit Ronald Reagan, George Shultz, Menachem Begin, Shimon Peres, and other voices of the emperor and his court to speak without rebuttal, advocating "low-intensity warfare" and "retaliation" or "pre-emption"? Are the media thereby permitting terrorist commanders free expression, thus serving as agents of wholesale terrorism? The question cannot be asked, and if raised, could only be dismissed with distaste or horror. The chapters that follow attempt to show that this reaction reflects the success of indoctrination, not understanding of the real world.

Literal censorship barely exists in the United States, but thought control is a flourishing industry, indeed an indispensable one in a society based on the principle of elite decision, public endorsement or passivity.

42

Notes

1   On the matters discussed here, see my *Towards a New Cold War* (Pantheon, 1982), particularly Chapters 1 and 2.

2.   Cited by Richard Fox, *Reinhold Niebuhr* (Pantheon, 1985), p. 138.

3.   John Dillin, *The Christian Science Monitor*, April 22, 1986.

4.   *The New York Times*, June 2, 1985.

5.   *Ibid.*, March 17, 1985.

6.   See my *Towards a New Cold War, op. cit.*, pp. 267, 300, 461; Noam Chomsky, *The Fateful Triangle: Israel, the United States, and the Palestinians* (Black Rose Books, 1984), pp. 67, 189.

7.   Yitzhak Rabin, *The Rabin Memoirs* (Little, Brown, 1979), p. 332. In keeping with his moderate stance, Rabin believes that the "refugees from the Gaza Strip and the West Bank" should be removed to East of the Jordan; see my *Towards a New Cold War, op. cit.*, p. 234, for representative quotes. On the longstanding Zionist conception of "transfer" of the indigenous population as a solution to the problem, and its current variants (e.g., the racist Rabbi Kahane or the American democratic socialist Michael Walzer, who suggests that those who are "marginal to the nation"—that is, Arab citizens of Israel—be "helped" to leave), see my *Fateful Triangle, op. cit.* The phrase "marginal to the nation" lifts the curtain on the essential contradiction between standard democratic principle and mainstream Zionism, and its realisation in Israel. See my *Towards a New Cold War, op. cit.*, and *The Fateful Triangle, op. cit.*, for discussion of this matter, which is close to unmentionable in the United States.

8.   Friedman provided serious and professional reporting from Lebanon during the 1982 war, and sometimes does from Israel as well; see, for example, his report on the Gaza Strip, April 5, 1986.

9.   Friedman, *The New York Times Magazine*, Oct. 7, 1984; *The New York Times*, March 17, 1985; editorial, *The New York Times*, March 21, 1985; and much other commentary and news reporting.

10. See Chapter 2, note 58 and text, for details. For more extensive discussion of the "peace process" and "rejectionism" in the non-Orwellian senses of these terms—that is, in the real world—and of the successful efforts of the indoctrination system to

eliminate the facts from history, see my *Fateful Triangle, op. cit.*, and for some updating, the references of Chapter 2, note 58.

11.   For more extensive discussion, see my review of Kissinger's memoirs, reprinted in *Towards a New Cold War. op. cit.*

12.   Eric Pace, *The New York Times*, Oct. 7, 1981.

13.   For discussion, see my *Turning the Tide: The U.S. and Latin America* (Black Rose Books, rev. ed., 1987); my essays in the "New Right in America" issue of *Psychohistory Review* (Lawrence Friedman, ed., forthcoming); Thomas W. Walker, ed., *Reagan vs. the Sandinistas* (Westview, forthcoming); and my introduction to Morris Morley and James Petras, *The Reagan Administration and Nicaragua* (Pamphlet Series, Institute for Media Analysis, New York, forthcoming). The need to obscure the plain facts is the major reason for a record of lying that is impressive even by the standards of violent states.

14.   On these matters, including the origins of the "strategic asset" concept, the post-1973 negotiations leading to Camp David, and the immediate U.S. actions to undermine the September 1982 "Reagan Plan" as well as the "Shultz Plan" for Lebanon a few months later, see my *Fateful Triangle, op. cit.* The reality, which was generally obvious at the time, is very different from official versions repeated by the media and most of scholarship, though sometimes partially acknowledged years later; see, for example, Chapter 2, note 47 and text.

15.   Rubinstein, *Davar*, Aug. 5, 1983.

16.   General (ret.) Mattityahu Peled, "American Jewry: 'More Israeli Than Israelis'," *New Outlook*, May-June 1975. See also Col. (ret.) Meir Pail, who condemns the "idolatrous cult-worship of a Jewish fortress-state" on the part of the American Jewish community, warning that by their rejectionism they "have transformed the State of Israel into a war-god similar to Mars,"a state that will be "a complex compound of the racist state structure of South Africa and the violent, terror-ridden social fabric of Northern Ireland," "an original contribution to the annals of 21st century political science: a unique kind of Jewish state that will be a cause for shame for every Jew wherever he may be, not only in the present, but in the future as well" ("Zionism in Danger of Cancer," *New Outlook*, Oct.-Dec. 1983, Jan. 1984).

17.   See my *Towards a New Cold War, op. cit.*, p. 247f., for details. On the new legislation, see Aryeh Rubinstein, *The Jerusalem Post*, Nov. 14, 1985. For some recent Israeli commentary, comparing Israeli laws and South African Apartheid, see Ori

Shohet, "No One Shall Grow Tomatoes…" *Ha'aretz Supplement*, Sept. 27, 1985 (translated in *News From Within* (Jerusalem), June 23, 1986), discussing the devices that ensure discrimination against Arab citizens of Israel and Arabs in the occupied territories with regard to land and other rights. The title refers to military regulations that require West Bank Arabs to obtain a license to plant a fruit tree or vegetables, one of the devices used to enable Israel to take over lands there on grounds of inadequate title.

18. Paul Berman, "The Anti-Imperialism of Fools," *The Village Voice*, April 22, 1986, citing "an inspired essay" by Bernard Lewis in *The New York Review* expounding this convenient doctrine. For some other ingenious applications of the concept of anti-Semitism, see my *Fateful Triangle. op. cit.*, p. 14f.

19. For discussion, see my *Towards a New Cold War. op. cit.*, and my *For Reasons of State* (Pantheon, 1973).

20. For discussion of these matters, see references of note 13. It is noteworthy that contributors who hold a more nuanced view did not express them in the opinion pieces that appeared in the U.S. national press.

21. Note that the point at issue is the permitted range of expression in the national forum, not the individual contributions, which are to be judged on their own merits.

22. See, for example, Timothy Garton Ash, "New Orthodoxies: I," *The Spectator* (London), July 19, 1986. The comical "debate" (in which only one side receives public expression despite elaborate pretense to the contrary) over "moral equivalence" in the U.S. merits a separate discussion.

23. *The New York Review of Books*, Aug. 14, 1986.

24. "Non-Orwellian Propaganda Systems," *Thoreau Quarterly*, Winter/Spring 1984. See my talk to a group of journalists reprinted here, and the ensuing discussion, for more on these topics.

25. Reich, *The New York Times*, July 24; Heller, *The New York Times*, June 10, 1986.

26. Anthony Lewis, *The New York Times*, April 21, 1986.

CHAPTER TWO
Middle East Terrorism and the American Ideological System

On October 17, 1985, President Reagan met in Washington with Israeli Prime Minister Shimon Peres, who told him that Israel was prepared to take "bold steps" in the Middle East and extend "the hand of peace" to Jordan.

"Mr. Peres's visit comes at a moment of unusual American-Israeli harmony," commented David Shipler in *The Times*, quoting a State Department official who described U.S. relations with Israel as "extraordinarily close and strong." And indeed, Peres was warmly welcomed by the American media as a man of peace, commended for his forthright commitment to "bear the cost of peace in preference to the price of war," in his words. The president said that he and Mr. Peres discussed "the evil scourge of terrorism, which has claimed so many Israeli, American, and Arab victims and brought tragedy to many others," adding that "we agreed that terrorism must not blunt our efforts to achieve peace in the Middle East."[1]

It would require the talents of a Jonathan Swift to do justice to this exchange between two of the world's leading terrorist commanders, whose shared conception of "peace," furthermore, excludes one of the two groups that claim the right of national self-determination in the former Palestine: the indigenous population.

The Jordan Valley is an "inseparable part of the State of Israel," declared Shimon Peres, the man of peace, while touring Israeli settlements there in 1985. This is consistent with his unwavering stand that "the past is immutable and the Bible is the decisive document in determining the fate of our land" and that a Palestinian state would "threaten Israel's very existence."[2] Peres's conception of a Jewish state, which is much lauded in the U.S. for its moderation, does not *threaten*, but rather *eliminates* the existence of the Palestinian people. But this consequence is considered of little moment, at worst a minor defect in an imperfect world.

Peres and other Israeli leaders have not moved an inch from the 1972 position of the current president, Chaim Herzog, that the Palestinians can never be "partners in any way in a land that has been holy to our people for thousands of years." The "doves," though, prefer to exclude West Bank areas of heavy Arab population from the Jewish state to avoid what they euphemistically term "the demographic problem."

Former chief of Israeli intelligence Shlomo Gazit, who was a senior military official from 1967 to 1973, observes that its basic principle was "that it is necessary to prevent the inhabitants of the [occupied] territories from participating in shaping the political future of the territory and they must not be seen as a partner for dealings with Israel"; hence "the absolute prohibition of any political organization, for it was clearly understood by everyone that if political activism and organization were permitted, its leaders would become potential participants in political affairs." The same considerations require "the destruction of all initiative and every effort on the part of the inhabitants of the territories to serve as a pipeline for negotiations, to be a channel to the Palestinian Arab leadership outside of the territories." Israeli policy is a "success story," Gazit concludes, because these goals, which persist to this day, have been achieved.

Israel's position, which has U.S. support, continues to be that of Prime Minister Yitzhak Rabin (now minister of defense), when in January 1976 the PLO and the Arab states

48

submitted a proposal to the United Nations for a peaceful two-state settlement: Israel will reject any negotiations with the PLO even if it recognises Israel and renounces terrorism, and will not enter into "political negotiations with Palestinians," PLO or not.[3]

Neither Peres nor Reagan have been willing even to consider the explicit proposals by the PLO—which they both know has overwhelming support among the Palestinians and has as much legitimacy as the Zionist organisation did in 1947—for negotiations leading to mutual recognition in a two-state settlement in accord with the broad international consensus that has been blocked at every turn by the U.S. and Israel for many years.[4]

These crucial political realities provide the necessary framework for any discussion of "the evil scourge of terrorism," which, in the racist terms of American discourse, refers to terrorist acts by Arabs, but not by Jews, just as "peace" means a settlement that honours the right of national self-determination of Jews, but not of Palestinians.

Peres arrived in Washington to discourse on peace and terrorism with his partner in crime directly after having sent his bombers to attack Tunis, where they killed twenty Tunisians and fifty-five Palestinians, Israeli journalist Amnon Kapeliouk reported from the scene. The target was undefended, "a vacation resort with several dozen homes, vacation cottages and PLO offices side by side and untermingled in such a way that even from close by it is difficult to distinguish" among them. The weapons were more sophisticated than those used in Beirut, "smart bombs" apparently, which crushed their targets to dust.

> The people who were in the bombed buildings were torn to shreds beyond recognition. They showed me a series of pictures of the dead. "You may take them," I was told. I left the pictures in the office. No newspaper in the world would publish terror photos such as these. I was told that a Tunisian boy who sold sandwiches near the headquarters was torn to pieces. His father identified the body by a scar on his ankle. "Some of the wounded were brought out from under the rubble, apparently

49

healthy and unhurt," my guide told me. "Half an hour later they collapsed in contortions and died. Apparently their internal organs had been destroyed from the power of the blast."[5]

Tunisia had accepted the Palestinians at Reagan's behest after they had been expelled from Beirut in a U.S.-supported invasion that left some twenty thousand people killed and much of the country destroyed. "You used a hammer against a fly," Israeli military correspondent Ze'ev Schiff was informed by "a leading Pentagon figure, a general who is familiar with the Israeli military (IDF) and several other armies of the region." "You struck many civilians without need. We were astounded by your attitude to the Lebanese civilians." This feeling was shared by Israeli soldiers and senior officers who were appalled at the savagery of the attack and the treatment of civilians and prisoners[6]—though support in Israel for the aggression and for the Begin-Sharon team increased parallel to the atrocities, reaching its very high peak after the terror bombing of Beirut in August.[7]

Shimon Peres, the man of peace and a respected figure in the Socialist International, kept his silence until the costs to Israel began to mount with the postwar Sabra-Shatila massacres and the toll taken by the Lebanese resistance. This undermined Israel's plan to establish a "New Order" in Lebanon with Israel in control of large areas of the south and the remnants ruled by Israel's Phalangist allies and selected Muslim elites.

There can be no doubt, Kapeliouk comments, that Arafat was the target of the Tunis attack. In the PLO office to which he was taken, a picture of Arafat stands amidst the ruins with the caption: "They wanted to kill me instead of negotiating with me."

"The PLO wishes negotiations," Kapeliouk was told, "but Israel rejects any discussion"—a simple statement of fact that was effectively concealed by the U.S. media, or, worse, dismissed as irrelevant given the guiding racist premises.

Neither can there be any serious doubt of U.S. complicity in the Tunis attack. The U.S. did not even warn the victims— close American allies—that the killers were on the way.

Anyone who credits the American pretense that the Sixth Fleet and the extensive U.S. surveillance system in the region were incapable of detecting the Israeli planes refueled en route over the Mediterranean should be calling for a Congressional investigation into American military competence, which surely leaves the U.S. and its allies wide open to enemy attack.

"News reports now quote government sources as saying the U.S. Sixth Fleet was undoubtedly aware of the coming raid but decided not to inform Tunisian officials," *The Los Angeles Times* reported, citing wire services. But "that very significant statement was not reported in the two major east coast papers, *The New York Times* and *The Washington Post*, nor in the other U.S. papers, nor was it used in the overseas service" of AP and UPI, London *Economist* Mideast correspondent Godfrey Jansen reported, adding that "U.S. passive collusion was absolutely certain."[8]

One of the victims of the Tunis bombing was Mahmoud el-Mughrabi, who was born in Jerusalem in 1960, was held under detention twelve times by the age of sixteen, and was one of the informants for *The London Sunday Times* investigation of torture in Israel (June 19, 1977). He "managed to escape to Jordan after years of increasingly marginal existence under steadily deteriorating conditions of the military occupation," said a memorial notice by Israeli Jewish friends that was repeatedly denied publication in Arab newspapers in East Jerusalem by Israeli military censorship.[9] These facts would, of course, be meaningless in the United States, if only because *The Sunday Times* study was largely excluded from the press, though it was noted in the liberal *New Republic*, along with an explicit defense of torture of Arabs that elicited no public reaction.[10]

The United States officially welcomed the Israeli bombing of Tunis as "a legitimate response" to "terrorist attacks." Secretary of State Shultz confirmed this judgement in a telephone call to Israeli Foreign Minister Yitzhak Shamir, informing him that the president and others "had considerable sympathy for the Israeli action," the press reported.[11]

The U.S. drew back from such open support after an adverse global reaction, but it abstained from the U.S. Security

Council condemnation of this "act of armed aggression" in "flagrant violation of the Charter of the United Nations, international law and norms of conduct"—standing alone as usual. The intellectual and cultural climate in the U.S. is reflected by the fact that this position was bitterly condemned as yet another instance of a "pro-PLO" and "anti-Israel" stance, and a refusal to strike hard at—carefully selected— terrorists.

One might argue that the Israeli bombing does not fall under the rubric of international terrorism because it is an instance of the far more serious crime of aggression, as the U.N. Security Council maintained. Or one might hold that it is unfair to apply to Israel the definition of "international terrorism" designed by others.

To counter the latter complaint, we may consider its own doctrine, as formulated by Ambassador Benjamin Netanyahu at an international conference on terrorism. The distinguishing factor in terrorism, he explained, is "deliberate and systematic murder and maiming [of civilians] designed to inspire fear."[12] Clearly, the Tunis attack and other Israeli atrocities over the years fall under this concept, though most acts of international terrorism do not, even the most outrageous terrorist attacks against Israelis (Ma'alot, the Munich macssacre, the coastal road atrocity of 1978 that provided the pretext for invading Lebanon, etc.), or even airplane hijacking or the taking of hostages generally, the very topic of the conference Netanyahu was attending.

The attack on Arafat's PLO headquarters was allegedly in retaliation for the murder of three Israelis in Larnaca, Cyprus, by assailants who were captured and faced trial for their crime. "Western diplomatic experts on the PLO" doubt that Arafat was aware of the planned mission, and "the Israelis, too, have dropped their original contention that Mr. Arafat had been involved."[13]

American apologists for Israeli terrorism are unimpressed. They assure us that "Israel's Tunisian raid precisely targeted people responsible for terrorist activities." Whatever the facts, they explain, "the larger moral responsibility for atrocities... is *all* Yasir Arafat's" because "he was, and remains, the founding father of contemporary Palestinian violence."

In an address to the Israeli lobbying group AIPAC, Attorney-General Edwin Meese stated that the U.S. will hold Arafat "accountable for acts of international terrorism" quite generally, facts apparently being irrelevant.[14] Therefore, any act "against the PLO"—a very broad category, as the historical record demonstrates—is legitimate.

The Tunis attack was consistent with Israeli practice since the earliest days of the state: retaliation is directed against those who are vulnerable, not against the perpetrators of atrocities. A standard condemnation of the PLO is that "instead of directly attacking security-minded foes like Israel, for example, Palestinians have attacked softer Israeli targets in Italy, Austria, and elsewhere"[15]—another sign of their vile and cowardly nature. The similar Israeli practice, which was initiated long before and is vastly greater in scale, escapes notice in the midst of the general praise for Israeli heroism, military efficiency, and "purity of arms." The concept of "retaliation" also raises more than a few questions, a matter to which we turn directly.

As 1985 came to an end, the press reviewed the record of "a year of bloody international terrorism," including the murders in Larnaca on September 25 and the *Achille Lauro* hijacking and murder of an American tourist on October 7. Israel's October 1 attack was not included on the list. In its lengthy year-end review of terrorism, *The Times* briefly notes the Tunis bombing, but as an example of retaliation, not terrorism, describing it as "an act of desperation that had little effect on Palestinian violence and provoked an outcry by other nations."

Harvard law professor Alan Dershowitz, condemning Italy for complicity in international terrorism by releasing the man "who allegedly masterminded the hijacking," observed that the U.S. "would certainly extradite any Israeli terrorist who had done violence to citizens of another country"—Ariel Sharon, Yitzhak Shamir, or Menachem Begin, for example. This statement appeared on the very day that Shimon Peres was being feted in Washington immediately after the Tunis bombing and lauded for his commitment to peace, and is considered entirely natural in the prevailing cultural climate.[16]

Reagan's pronouncements on terrorism are reported and discussed with apparent seriousness in the mainstream. Critics have occasionally remarked, however, on the hypocrisy of those who fulminate about international terrorism while sending their client armies to murder, mutilate, torture, and destroy in Nicaragua and—this is less commonly noted, since these acts are considered a grand success—to massacre tens of thousands in El Salvador in a determined and successful effort to avert the dread threat of meaningful democracy there. Reagan is a latecomer on the scene, though, and cannot claim to be among "the founding fathers of contemporary Central American terrorism" in Washington.

Shortly after the Reagan-Peres discourse on peace and terror, a group of 120 doctors, nurses, and other health professionals returned from an investigation in Nicaragua that was endorsed by the American Public Health Association and the World Health Organization. They reported the destruction of clinics and hospitals, the murder of health professionals, the looting of rural pharmacies leading to a critical shortage of medicines, and the successful disruption of a polio vaccination programme, one small part of a campaign of violence organised in the centres of international terrorism in Washington and Miami.[17] *Times* reporters in Nicaragua match their *Pravda* colleagues in Afghanistan in their zeal to unearth or check the overwhelming evidence of *contra* atrocities, and this report, like many others, was ignored in the Newspaper of Record.

The raid near Tunis yields a measure of the hypocrisy, which is not always easy to grasp. Suppose Nicaragua were to carry out bombings in Washington aimed at Reagan, Shultz, and other international terrorists, killing some hundred thousand people "by accident." This would be entirely justified retaliation by American standards, if indeed a ratio of twenty-five to one is acceptable, as in the Larnaca-Tunis exchange, though we might add for accuracy that in this case at least the perpetrators would be targeted and there is no question about who initiated the terror, and perhaps the appropriate number of deaths should be multiplied by some factor in consideration of the relative population sizes.

"Terrorists, and those who support them, must, and will, be held to account," President Reagan declared,[18] thus providing the moral basis for any such act of retaliation. His harshest critics in the mainstream press are in full accord, as we have seen.

Peres had already distinguished himself as a man of peace in Lebanon.[19] After he became prime minister, Israel's "counterterror" programmes against civilians in occupied southern Lebanon intensified, reaching their peak of savagery with the Iron Fist operations of early 1985, which had "the earmarks of Latin American death squads," Curtis Wilkie commented, affirming reports of other journalists on the scene.

In the village of Zrariya, for exmaple, the IDF, pursuing its vocation of "purity of arms," carried out an operation well to the north of its then-current frontline. After several hours of heavily shelling Zrariya and three nearby villages, the IDF carted off the entire male population, killing thirty-five to forty villagers, some in cars crushed by Israeli tanks; other villagers were beaten or simply murdered, and a tank shell was fired at Red Cross workers who were warned to stay away. Israeli troops miraculously escaped without casualties from what was officially described as a gun battle with heavily-armed guerrillas.

The day before, twelve Israeli soldiers had been killed in a suicide attack near the border, but Israel denied that the attack on Zrariya was retaliation. The Israeli denial is dutifully presented as fact by apologists in the United States, who explain that "intelligence had established that the town had become a base for terrorists.... No less than 34 Shiite guerrillas were killed in the gun battle and more than 100 men were taken away for questioning—from one small village" (Eric Breindel), which indicates the scale of the Shi'ite terror network. Being unaware of the party line, Israeli soldiers painted the slogan "Revenge of the Israeli Defense Forces" in Arabic on the walls of the town, reporters on the scene observed.[20]

Elsewhere, Israeli gunners shot at hospitals and schools and took "suspects"—including patients in hospital beds and operating rooms—for "interrogation" or to Israeli concentration camps. Such atrocities were described by a Western diplomat who often travels in the area as reaching new depths of "calculated brutality and arbitrary murder."[21]

The head of the IDF liaison unit in Lebanon, General Shlomo Ilya, "said the only weapon against terrorism is terrorism and that Israel has options beyond those already used for 'speaking the language the terrorists understand'."

This concept is not a novel one. Gestapo operations in occupied Europe also "were justified in the name of combatting 'terrorism'." One of Klaus Barbie's murder victims was found with a note pinned to his chest reading "Terror Against Terror"—incidentally, the name adopted by an Israeli terrorist group and the heading of a *Der Spiegel* cover story on the U.S. terror bombing of Libya in April 1986.

A U.N. Security Council resolution calling for condemnation of "Israeli practices and measures against the civilian population in southern Lebanon" was vetoed by the United States on the grounds that it "applies double standards"; "We don't believe an unbalanced resolution will end the agony of Lebanon," Jeane Kirkpatrick explained.[22]

Israel's terror operations continued as its forces were compelled to withdraw by the resistance.

To mention only one case, Israeli troops and their South Lebanon Army (SLA) mercenaries brought the "year of bloody international terrorism" to an end on December 31, 1985, as they "stormed a Shiite Moslem village [Kunin] in southern Lebanon and forced its entire population of about 2,000 to leave." They blew up houses, set others on fire, and rounded up thirty-two young men; old men, women, and children from the village were reported to be streaming into a town outside the Israeli "security zone," where the U.N. force had a command post.[23]

This report, which is based on witnesses' accounts quoted by the Lebanese police, a journalist from the conservative Beirut journal *An Nahar*, and the Shi'ite Amal movement, was filed from Beirut. From Jerusalem, Joel Greenberg provides a different version, not on the basis of any identified sources, but as simple fact: "Villagers fearful of an SLA reprisal fled the Shiite village of Kunin after two SLA soldiers were slain in the village."[24]

The comparison, which is typical, is instructive. Israeli propaganda benefits greatly from the fact that the media rely overwhelmingly on Israel-based correspondents. This yields two crucial advantages: first, the "news" is presented to the American audience through official Israeli eyes; second, on the rare occasions when U.S. correspondents carry out independent inquiry instead of simply relying on their genial hosts, the Israeli propaganda system and its numerous U.S. affiliates can complain bitterly that Arab crimes are ignored while Israel is subjected to detailed scrutiny for any minor imperfection, given the density of reporting.

Inability to manage the news in the usual fashion sometimes creates problems. During the 1982 Lebanon war, for example, Israel had no way of controlling the eyewitness reports by Lebanon-based journalists. There was a huge outcry over alleged atrocity-mongering and fabrication in a "broad-scale mass psychological war" waged against pitiful little Israel, another sign of the inveterate anti-Semitism of world opinion; Israel became the victim, not the aggressor. It is easily demonstrated that the charges are false, often merely comical, and that the media predictably bent over backwards to see things from the Israeli point of view—not an easy matter for journalists attempting to survive Israeli terror bombing. In fact, testimony from Israeli sources was often far harsher than what was reported in the U.S. press, and what appeared in U.S. journals was often a considerably watered-down version of what journalists actually perceived.[25] But the charges are taken very seriously despite their manifest absurdity, while accurate critique of the media for its subordination to the U.S.-Israeli perspective and suppression of unacceptable facts is, as usual, entirely ignored.

Typically, the study "Published Analyses of Media Coverage of the 1982 War in Lebanon" includes numerous denunciations of the press for an alleged anti-Israel stance and a few defenses of the media against these charges, but not even a reference to the fact that there were extensive, and quite accurate, critical analyses of exactly the opposite phenomenon.[26] Within

57

the narrow constraints of the highly ideological U.S. intellectual climate, only the former criticism can even be heard. This is, incidentally, a typical phenomenon, one easily demonstrated in connection with the Indochina wars and the current Central America wars, and serving as yet another device of thought control.

The Iron Fist operations, which the Israeli command is happy to describe as "terrorism" (see General Ilya's remarks, cited above), had two main purposes. The first, John Kifner observes (from Lebanon), was "to turn the population against the guerrillas by making the cost of supporting them too high; in short, to hold the population hostage to terrorist attack, unless they accept the arrangements Israel intends to impose by force.

The second aim of the Iron Fist operations was to exacerbate internal conflicts in Lebanon and to implement a general population exchange after intercommunal strife, much of which appears to have been incited by the occupier since 1982, in the classic manner.

"There is a great deal of evidence," Lebanon-based correspondent Jim Muir observes, "that the Israelis helped fuel and encourage the Christian-Druze conflict" in the Chouf region. In the south, a senior international aid official said: "Their dirty tricks department did everything it could to stir up trouble, but it just didn't work." That "their behaviour was wicked" is a view "shared by the international relief community as a whole." "Local eyewitnesses reported that Israeli soldiers frequently shot into the Palestinian camps from nearby Christian areas in an effort to incite the Palestinians against the Christians." Residents of the Christian villages reported that Israeli patrols forced Christians and Muslims at gunpoint to punch one another and to submit to other forms of "bizarre humiliation."

The techniques finally worked. Israel's Christian allies attacked Muslims near Sidon in a manner guaranteed to elicit a response from considerably more powerful forces, initiating a bloody cycle of violence that ultimately led to the flight of tens of thousands of Christians, many to the Israeli-dominated regions in the south, while tens of thousands of Shi'ites were driven north by the Iron Fist operations.[27]

The pretense in the United States was that Israel was always planning to withdraw, so that the Shi'ite terrorists were simply indulging in the usual Arab pleasure in violence for its own sake, delaying the planned withdrawal. But as Jim Muir correctly observes, "it is a historical fact beyond serious dispute that the Israelis would not be withdrawing now were it not for the attacks and the casualties they have caused," and the extent of the withdrawal could be determined by the intensity of the resistance.[28]

The Israeli high command explained that the victims of the Iron Fist operations were "terrorist villagers." It was thus understandable that thirteen villagers were massacred by SLA militiamen in the incident that elicited this observation. Yossi Olmert of the Shiloah Institute, Israel's institute of strategic studies, observed that "these terrorists operate with the support of most of the local population." An Israeli commander complained that "the terrorist... has many eyes here, because he lives here," while the military correspondent of *The Jerusalem Post* described the problems faced in combatting the "terrorist mercenary": "fanatics, all of whom are sufficiently dedicated to their causes to go on running the risk of being killed while operating against the IDF," which must "maintain order and security" despite "the price the inhabitants will have to pay," arousing his "admiration for the way in which they were doing their job."

Leon Wieseltier explained the difference between "Shiite terrorism" against the occupying army and Palestinian terrorism, each a manifestation of the evil Arab nature: "The Palestinians had murderers who wished to kill. The Shiites have murderers who wish to die," conducting actions "inspired by a chiliastic demand of the world for which there can be no merely political or diplomatic satisfaction"—nothing so simple as removing the occupying army from their land. Rather, their "secret army" Amal has been "consecrated" to "the destruction of Israel" since its founding in 1975—manifest nonsense that goes well beyond the tales concocted by his mentors.[29]

The same concept of terrorism is widely used by U.S. officials and commentators. Thus the press reports, without comment, that Secretary of State Shultz's concern over "international terrorism" became "his passion" after the suicide bombing of U.S. Marines in Lebanon in October 1983, troops that much of the population saw, quite naturally, as a foreign military force sent to impose the "New Order" established by the Israeli aggression. Barry Rubin writes that "the most important use of Syrian-sponsored terrorism within Lebanon was to force the withdrawal of Israeli troops and U.S. Marines," while both Iran and Syria have supported "terrorist activity" by "Shiite extremist groups" in southern Lebanon, such as attacks on "the Israeli-backed South Lebanese army." For the apologist for state terror, resistance to an occupying army or its local mercenaries is terrorism, meriting harsh reprisal.

Times Israel correspondent Thomas Friedman routinely describes attacks in southern Lebanon directed against Israeli forces as "terrorist bombings" or "suicide terrorism," which, he assures us, is the product of "psychological weaknesses or religious fervor." He reports further that residents of Israel's "security zone" who violate the rules established by the occupiers are "shot on the spot, with questions asked later. Some of those shot have been innocent bystanders." But this is not state terrorism. Friedman also notes that Israel "has taken great pains to limit the flow of news out of the area": "No reporters have been allowed to cover the aftermaths of suicide attacks, and virtually no information is released about them." Yet this does not prevent him from reporting with much confidence about the background and motives of those designated "terrorists" by the occupiers— hence in his news reports as well.[30]

As Reagan and Peres were congratulating one another on their principled stand against "the evil scourge of terrorism" before their admiring audience, the press reported yet another terrorist act in southern Lebanon: "Terrorists Kill 6, Demolish U.S.-Owned Christian Radio Station in S. Lebanon," the headlines read on the same day.[31] Why should Lebanese terrorists destroy the "Voice of Hope," run by American Christian missionaries? The question was barely raised, but let us look into it, in the interest of clarifying the concepts of terrorism and retaliation.

One reason is that the station "speaks for the South Lebanon Army,"[32] the mercenary force established by Israel in southern Lebanon to terrorise the population in its "security zone." The location of the station, near the village of Khiam, is also worthy of note. Khiam's history is unknown in the United States. Ze'ev Schiff alluded to this history in the midst of Peres's Iron Fist operations. He observed that when Israel invaded Lebanon in 1982, the village of Khiam was "empty of inhabitants," although now it has ten thousand people, and that the Lebanese town of Nabatiya had only five thousand inhabitants, today fifty thousand. "These and others will once again be forced to abandon their homes if they permit extremists in their community or Palestinians to attack Israeli settlements," Schiff explained.[33] That will be their fate if they mimic the IDF, which was then attacking Lebanese villages and randomly murdering civilians in defense against the "terrorism [that] has not disappeared" as "Israeli soldiers are harrassed daily in southern Lebanon."[34]

For the Lebanese to whom the warning was addressed, and for at least some better-informed elements of his Israeli audience, Schiff did not have to explain why the population of Nabatiya had been reduced to five thousand and Khiam had been emptied by 1982. The population had been driven out, with hundreds killed, by Israeli terror bombardment from the early 1970s. The handful who had remained in Khiam were slaughtered during the 1978 invasion of Lebanon, under the eyes of the elite Golani brigade, by Israel's Haddad militia, which "succeeded in establishing relative peace in the region and preventing the return of PLO terrorists," the man of peace explained.[35]

Khiam is also the site of a "secret jail" maintained by "Israel and its local militia allies in south Lebanon... where detainees are held in appalling conditions and subjected to beatings and electric-shock torture, according to former inmates and international relief officials in the area." The Red Cross reported that "Israelis were running the center" and that it had been refused entry by the IDF.[36]

There might have been more to say, then, about the terrorist attack by "fanatics" at Khiam on October 17, 1985, were matters such as these considered fit to become part of

61

historical memory alongside other acts of terror of greater ideological serviceability.

Nabatiya, too, has further stories to tell. The flight of fifty thousand of its sixty thousand people "mostly because of fear of the [Israeli] shelling" was reported by two *Jerusalem Post* correspondents who were touring southern Lebanon in an effort to unearth evidence of PLO terror and atrocities, finding little, though there was ample evidence of Israeli terror and its effects.[37] One such bombardment took place on November 4, 1977, when Nabatiya "came under heavy artillery fire from [Israeli-supported] Lebanese Maronite positions and also from Israeli batteries on both sides of the frontier—including some of the six Israeli strongpoints inside Lebanon." The attacks continued the next day, killing three women and causing other casualties. On November 6, two rockets fired by Fatah guerrillas killed two Israelis in Nahariya, setting off an artillery battle and a second rocket attack that killed one Israeli. "Then came the Israeli air raids in which some 70 people, nearly all Lebanese, were killed."[38] This Israeli-initiated exchange, which threatened to cause a major war, was cited by Egyptian President Sadat as a reason for his offer to visit Jerusalem a few days later.[39]

These events have entered historical memory in a different form, however, not only in journalism but also in scholarship: "In an effort to disrupt the movement towards a peace conference," Edward Haley writes on the basis of no evidence, "the PLO fired Katyusha rockets into the northern Israeli village of Nahariya, on November 6 and 8, killing three" and eliciting "the inevitable Israeli reprisal" on November 9, with more than one hundred people killed in attacks "in and around Tyre and two small towns to the south."[40] As is the rule in properly sanitised history, Palestinians carry out terrorism, Israelis then retaliate, perhaps too harshly. In the real world, the truth is often rather different, a matter of no small significance for the study of terrorism in the Middle East.

The torment of Nabatiya was noted little in the Western press, though there are a few exceptions. One of the Israeli attacks took place on December 2, 1975, when the Israeli air force bombed the town—killing many Lebanese and

Palestinian civilians—using antipersonnel weapons, bombs, and rockets.[41] This raid, which was unusual in that it was reported, aroused no interest or concern in civilised circles, perhaps because it was apparently a "retaliation": namely, retaliation against the U.N. Security Council, which had just agreed to devote a session to the peace offer by Syria, Jordan, Egypt, and the PLO discussed in Chapter One.

The story continues almot unchanged today. In early 1986, while the eyes of the world were focused in horror on the lunatic terrorists in the Arab world, the press reported that Israeli tank cannon poured fire into the village of Sreifa in southern Lebanon, aiming at thirty houses from which the IDF claimed they had been fired upon by "armed terrorists" resisting their military actions in the course of what they described as a search for two Israeli soldiers who had been "kidnapped" in the Israeli "security zone" in Lebanon.

Largely kept from the American press was the report by the U.N. peace-keeping forces that Israeli troops "went really crazy" in these operations, locking up entire villages, preventing the U.N. troops from sending in water, milk, and oranges to the villagers subjected to "intetrrogation"— meaning brutal torture of men and women by Israeli forces and their local mercenaries with IDF troops standing by. The IDF then departed, taking away many villagers (including pregnant women)—some of whom were brought to Israel in further violation of international law—destroying houses and looting others. Shimon Peres, meanwhile, said that Israel's search for its "kidnapped" soldiers "expresses our attitude towards the value of human life and dignity."[42]

A month later, on March 24, Lebanese radio reported that Israeli forces, either IDF or SLA mercenaries, shelled Nabatiya, killing three civilians and wounding twenty-two. "Shells slammed into the marketplace in the center of town at daybreak as crowds gathered for trading," allegedly in retaliation for an attack on Israel's mercenary forces in southern Lebanon.

A leader of the Shi'ite Amal vowed that "Israeli settlements and installatións will not be beyond the blows of the resistance." On March 27, a Katyusha rocket struck a schoolyard in northern Israel, injuring five people and eliciting an Israeli attack on Palestinian refugee camps near Sidon, killing ten people and wounding twenty-two, while Israel's northern commander stated over Israeli army radio that the IDA had not determined whether the rocket had been fired by Shi'ite or Palestinian guerrillas. On April 7, Israeli planes bombed the same camps and a neighbouring village, killing two and wounding twenty, claiming that terrorists had set out from there with the intent of killing Israeli citizens.[43]

Of all these events, only the rocket attack on northern Israel merited anguished TV coverage and general outrage at "the evil scourge of terrorism." This was somewhat muted, though, because of the mass hysteria then being orchestrated over a Nicaraguan "invasion" of Honduras, as the Nicaraguan army exercised its legal right of hot pursuit in driving out of its territory terrorist gangs dispatched by their U.S. directors in a show of force just prior to the Senate vote on *contra* aid; recall that the only serious issue under debate in the terrorist state is whether the proxy army can accomplish the goals assigned them by their master.[44]

Israel, of course, was not exercising a legal right of hot pursuit in shelling and bombing towns and refugee camps, nor have its acts of wholesale terrorism and outright aggression in Lebanon ever fallen under this concept. But as a client state, Israel inherits from the emperor the right of terrorism, torture, and aggression. And Nicaragua, as an enemy, plainly lacks the right to defend its territory from U.S. international terrorism, though one might argue that U.S. actions there reach the level of aggression, a war crime of the category for which people were hanged at Nuremberg and Tokyo. Consequently, it is natural that Israel's actions should be ignored, or dismissed as legitimate "retaliation," while Congress, across the narrow spectrum, denounced the "Nicaraguan Marxist-Leninists" for this renewed demonstration of the threat they pose to regional peace and stability.

The Israeli invasion of Lebanon in June 1982, too, is regularly presented in properly sanitised form. Shimon Peres writes that the "Peace for Galilee" operation was fought "in order to ensure that the Galilee will no longer be shelled by Katyusha-rocket attacks and other shelling from Lebanon." The news pages of *The Times* inform us that the invasion began "after attacks by Palestine Liberation Organization guerrillas on Israel's northern settlements," and (without comment) that Israeli leaders "said they wanted to end the rocket and shelling attacks on Israel's northern border," which "has been accomplished for the three years the Israeli army has spent in Lebanon." Adds Henry Kamm:

> For nearly three years, the peoople of Qiryat Shemona have not slept in their bomb shelters, and parents have not worried when their children went out to school or to play. The Soviet-made Katyusha rockets, which for many years struck this town near the Lebanese border at random intervals, have not fallen since Israel invaded Lebanon in June 1982.

And Thomas Friedman observes that

> if rockets again rain down on Israel's northern border after all that has been expended on Lebanon, the Israeli public will be outraged; ...right now there are no rockets landing in northern Israel... and if large-scale attacks begin afresh on Israel's northern border that minority [that favours keeping the army in Lebanon] could grow into a majority again.

"Operation Peace for Galilee—the Israeli invasion of Lebanon—was originally undertaken" to protect the civilian population from Palestinian gunners, Friedman reports in one of the numerous human interest stories on the travail of the Israelis. Political figures regularly expound the same doctrine. Zbigniew Brzezinski writes that "the increased Syrian military presence and the use of Lebanon by the Palestine Liberation Organization for incursions against Israel precipitated the Israeli invasion last year." Ronald Reagan, in a typical display of moral cowardice, asks us to "remember that when this [the invasion] all started, Israel, because of the violations of its own northern border by the Palestinians, the PLO, had gone all the way to Beirut," where it was "10,000 Palestinians [!] who had been bringing ruin down on Beirut," not the mad bombers whom he was joyously supporting.[45]

These and innumerable other accounts, many with heart-rending descriptions of the torment of the people of the Galilee subjected to random Katyusha bombardment, help create the approved picture of Soviet-armed Palestinian fanatics, the central component of the Russian-based international terror network, who compel Israel to invade and strike Palestinian refugee camps and other targets, as any state would do, to defend its people from merciless terrorist attack.

The real world, once again, is rather different. David Shipler writes that "in the four years between the previous Israeli invasion of southern Lebanon in 1978 and the invasion of June 6, 1982, a total of 29 people were killed in northern Israel in all forms of attacks from Lebanon, including shelling and border crossings by terrorists," but that for a year before the 1982 invasion, "the border was quiet."[46]

This report has the merit of approaching at least half-truth. While the PLO refrained from cross-border actions for a year prior to the Israeli invasion, the border was far from quiet, since Israeli terror continued, killing many civilians; the border was "quiet" only in the racist term of U.S. discourse, once again. Furthermore, neither Shipler nor his associates recall that while twenty-nine people were killed in northern Israel from 1978, thousands were killed by Israeli bombardments in Lebanon, a fact which was barely noted in the United States, and in no sense was it "retaliatory."

The bombardments from 1978 were a central element of the Camp David "peace process," which, quite predictably, freed Israel to extend its takeover and repression in the occupied territories while attacking its northern neighbour, with the main Arab deterrent (Egypt) now removed from the conflict and U.S. military support rapidly increasing. William Quandt notes further that "the Israeli operational planning for the invasion of Lebanon against the PLO [in 1981-82] seems to coincide with the consolidation of the Egyptian-Israeli peace treaty."

It should be noted that the obvious significance of the Camp David agreements, although it was inexpressible in the U.S. media at the time (when it was equally obvious) and since, is understood by competent American journalists. Thus in an interview in Israel, David Shipler said:

> On the Israeli side, it seems to me that the peace treaty set up the situation for the war in Lebanon. With Egypt no longer a confrontation state, Israel felt free to initiate a war in Lebanon, something it probably would not have dared to do before the peace treaty... It is an irony [*sic*] that the war in Lebanon could not have taken place without the peace treaty.[17]

He wrote nothing of the sort in *The Times*, during his five years as its correspondent in Israel ending in June 1984, or since. Shipler added, "I think there would not have been such tremendous opposition to the war among Israelis without this same peace treaty." Having been in Israel at the time, he knows that the "tremendous opposition to the war" is a *post hoc* propaganda fabrication designed to restore the image of "the beautiful Israel." Opposition was in fact slight until the postwar Sabra-Shatila massacres (when American supporters of the war also deserted the sinking ship, constructing a fraudulent history of "earlier opposition," much as in the case of the Indochina war) and particularly the mounting costs of the occupation.[48]

Turning to the real world, consider first the immediate background of the "Peace for Galilee" operation. The PLO observed the U.S.-arranged ceasefire of July 1981 despite repeated Israeli efforts to evoke some action that could be used as a pretext for the planned invasion—bombardment in late April 1982, killing two dozen people, sinking of fishing boats, etc. The only exceptions were a light retaliation in May after Israeli bombardment, and the response to heavy Israeli bombing and ground attacks in Lebanon in June that caused many civilian casualties. The Israeli attacks were in "retaliation" for the attempted assassination of the Israeli ambassador in London by Abu Nidal, a sworn enemy of the PLO who did not even have an office in Lebanon—again, the familiar story of "retaliation."

It was this assassination attempt that was used as a pretext for the long-planned invasion.

The New Republic tells us that the successes of U.N. negotiator Brian Urquhart "have been minor, somehow forgettable: his negotiation of a PLO cease-fire [*sic*] in southern Lebanon in 1981, for instance."[49] That strict party-line journals should prefer to "forget" the facts is not surprising, but the prevalence of such convenient lapses of memory is noteworthy.

Furthermore, a look at what happened in July 1981 reveals the same pattern. On May 28, Ze'ev Schiff and Ehud Ya'ari write, Prime Minister Menachem Begin and Chief-of-Staff Rafael Eitan "took another step that would bring their country appreciably closer to a war in Lebanon with an action that was essentially calculated towards that end"; namely, they broke the ceasefire by bombing "PLO concentrations" (a term of Newspeak, referring to any target Israel chooses to hit) in southern Lebanon. The attacks continued from air and sea until June 3, Schiff and Ya'ari continue, while "the Palestinians responded gingerly for fear that a vigorous reaction would only provoke a crushing Israeli ground operation." A ceasefire was again established, broken again by Israel on July 10 with renewed bombardments. This time there was a Palestinian reaction, with rocket attacks that caused panic in the northern Galilee followed by heavy Israeli bombing of Beirut and other civilian targets. By the time a ceasefire was declared on July 24, some 450 Arabs—nearly all Lebanese civilians—and six Israelis were killed.[50]

Of this story, all that is remembered is the torment of the northern Galilee, subjected to random Katyusha bombing by PLO terrorists that finally provoked Israel to retaliate in its June 1982 invasion of Lebanon.

This is true even of serious journalists who do not simply provide a pipeline for official propaganda. Edward Walsh writes that "the repeated rocket attacks in 1981 had put [Qiryat Shemona] once again under siege," describing the "distraught parents" and the terror caused by "the pounding of artillery and rocket barrages from the nearby Palestinian bases," with no further word on what was happening. Curtis Wilkie, one of the more sceptical and perceptive American journalists in the Middle East, writes that Qiryat Shemona "came under withering fire from Palestinian Liberation Organization forces in 1981; the rain of Soviet-made Katyusha rockets was so intense at one point that those residents who had not fled were forced to spend eight consecutive days and nights in bomb shelters"—again, with no further word on the reasons for this "withering fire" or on the mood in Beirut and other civilian areas where hundreds were killed in the murderous Israeli bombardment. Nor were these matters raised elsewhere.[51]

The example gives some further insight into the concept of "terrorism" and "retaliation," as conceived within the U.S. ideological system, and into the racist assumptions which, as a matter of course, exclude the suffering of the primary victims, who are Arab and hence less than human.

The official story that "the rocket and shelling attacks on Israel's northern border" were ended thanks to the "Peace for Galilee" operation (*The New York Times*, see above) is doubly false. First, the border was quiet for a year prior to the invasion apart from Israeli terror attacks and provocations, and the major rocket attacks, in July 1981, were a response to Israeli terror which exacted a toll almost a hundred times greater than the PLO response in this incident alone.

Second, in sharp contrast to the preceding period, rocket attacks began shortly after the invasion ended, from early 1983, and have continued since. A group of dissident Israeli journalists report that in a two-week period in September 1985, fourteen Katyusha rockets were fired at the Galilee. Furthermore, "terrorist attacks" increased by fifty percent in the West Bank in the months following the war, and by the end of 1983 had increased by seventy percent since the war in Lebanon, becoming a severe threat by 1985—not a surprising consequence of atrocities and the destruction of the civil society and political system of the Palestinians.[52]

The real reason for the 1982 invasion was not the threat to the northern Galilee, as the sanitised history would have it, but rather the opposite, as was plausibly explained by Israel's leading specialist on the Palestinians, Hebrew University professor Yehoshua Porath (a "moderate" in Israeli parlance, who supports the Labour Party's "Jordanian solution" for the Palestinians), shortly after the invasion was launched.

The decision to invade, Porath suggests, "flowed from the very fact that the cease-fire had been observed." This was a "veritable catastrophe" for the Israeli government, because it threatened the policy of evading a political settlement. "The government's hope," he continued, "is that the stricken PLO, lacking a logistic and territorial base, will return to its earlier terrorism; it will carry out bombings throughout the world, hijack airplanes, and murder many Israelis," and thus "will lose part of the political legitimacy it has gained" and "undercut the danger" of negotiations with representative Palestinians, which would threaten the policy—shared by both major political groupings—of keeping effective control over the occupied territories.[53]

The plausible assumption of the Israeli leadership was that those who shape public opinion in the United States—the only country that counts, now that Israel has chosen to become a mercenary state serving the interests of its provider—could be counted on to obliterate the actual history and portray the terrorist acts resulting from Israeli aggression and atrocities as random acts of violence ascribable to defects in Arab character and culture, if not racial deficiencies.

Subsequent U.S. commentary on terrorism fulfills these natural expectations with some precision, a major propaganda coup for state terrorists in Jerusalem and Washington.

The basic points are understood well enough in Israel. Prime Minister Yitzhak Shamir stated over Israeli television that Israel went to war because there was "a terrible danger... not so much a military one as a political one."

This prompted the fine Israeli satirist B. Michael to write that "the lame excuse of a military danger or a danger to the Galilee is dead.... [We] have removed the political danger" by striking first, in time; now, "thank God, there is no one to talk to."

Columnist Aaron Bachar commented that "it is easy to understand the mood of the Israeli leadership. Arafat has been accused of steadily moving towards some kind of political accommodation with Israel" and "in the eyes of the Israeli Administration, this is the worst possible threat"—in the eyes of Labour as well as Likud.

Benny Morris observed that "the PLO held its fire along the northern border for a whole year, on a number of occasions omitting completely to react to Israeli actions (designed specifically to draw PLO fire on the North)," commenting further that for the senior IDF officers "the war's inevitability rested on the PLO as a political threat to Israel and to Israel's hold on the occupied territories," since "Palestinian hopes inside and outside the occupied territories for the maturation of nationalist aspirations rested on and revolved about the PLO." Like every sane commentator, he ridicules the hysterical talk about captured weapons and the PLO military threat, and predicts that "the Shi'ites of West Beirut, many of them refugees from previous Israeli bombardments of southern Lebanon in the 1970s, will probably remember the IDF siege of June-August [1982] for a long time," with long-term repercussions in "Shi'ite terrorism against Israeli targets."[54]

On the right wing, Likud Knesset Member Ehud Olmert commented that "the danger posed by the PLO to Israel did not lie in its extremism, but in the fictitious moderation Arafat managed to display without even losing sight of his ultimate aim, which is the destruction of Israel." (This is arguably true, in the sense in which David Ben-Gurion, while in power, never lost sight of his ultimate aim of expanding to "the limits of Zionist aspirations," including much of the surrounding countries and on some occasions the "biblical border" from the Nile to Iraq, while the native population would somehow be transferred.) A former West Bank administrator, Professor Menachem Milson, stated that "it is a mistake to think that the threat to Israel represented by the PLO is essentially a military one; rather, it is a political and ideological one."

Defense Minister Ariel Sharon explained just before the invasion that "quiet on the West Bank" requires "the destruction of the PLO in Lebanon." His ultra-right cohort, Chief-of-Staff Rafael Eitan, commented afterwards that the war was a success because it severely weakened "the political status" of the PLO and "the struggle of the PLO for a Palestinian state" while enforcing Israel's capacity "to block any such purpose."

Commenting on these statements, Israeli miltiary historian Uri Milshtein (a supporter of Labour's "Jordanian solution") observes that among the goals of the invasion in the Sharon-Eitan conception were: "to establish a New Order[55] in Lebanon and the Middle East"; "to advance the process of Sadatization in several Arab states"; "to guarantee the annexation of Judea and Samaria [the West Bank] to the state of Israel"; and "perhaps a solution of the Palestinian problem."

At the other end of the political spectrum, Knesset Member Amnon Rubinstein, who is much admired in the United States for his liberal and dovish stance, writes that even though the ceasefire had been observed "more or less" (to translate: observed by the PLO but not by Israel), the invasion of Lebanon was "justified" because of a potential, not actual, military threat: the arms and ammunition in southern Lebanon were intended for eventual use against Israel. Consider the implications of this astonishing argument in other contexts, even if we were to take seriously the claims about a potential PLO military threat to Israel.[56]

Note that Rubinstein anticipated the interesting doctrine enunciated by the Reagan Administration in justifying its April 1986 bombing of Libya in "self-defense against future attack," a matter to which we turn in the next chapter.

American apologists for Israeli atrocities occasionally acknowledge the same truths. Just before the invasion, *New Republic* editor Martin Peretz, echoing Sharon and Eitan, urged that Israel administer to the PLO a "lasting military defeat" in Lebanon that "will clarify to the Palestinians in the West Bank that their struggle for an independent state has suffered a setback of many years," so that "the Palestinians will be turned into just another crushed nation, like the Kurds or the Afghans." And Democratic Socialist Michael Walzer, who sees the solution for Palestinian Arabs — within Israel as well — in transfer of those "marginal to the nation" (essentially, the position of the racist Rabbi Kahane; see Chapter One, note 7), explained in *The New Republic* after the war: "I certainly welcome the political *defeat* of the PLO, and I believe that the limited military operation required to inflict that defeat can be defended under the theory of just war."[57]

72

It is intriguing, incidentally, to see the convergence on these issues of the Israeli ultra-right and American left-liberalism.

In short, the goals of the war were political, the occupied territories being one prime target, the "New Order" in Lebanon (and perhaps beyond) being another. The tale about protecting the border from terrorism is agitprop, eagerly swallowed by the docile U.S. media. If Palestinian terrorism can be revived, so much the better. And if we can't pin the blame on Arafat, he can at least be stigmatised as "the founding father of contemporary Palestinian violence" (*The New Republic*) so that his efforts at political settlement can be evaded.

The problem of evading a political settlement did not end with the destruction of the political base for the PLO, as had been hoped. The U.S. media must therefore remain vigilant to combat the threat and defend the doctrinal truth that the U.S. and Israel seek peace but are blocked by Arab rejectionism.

In April-May 1984, Arafat made a series of statements in Europe and Asia calling for negotiations with Israel leading to mutual recognition. The offer was immediately rejected by Israel, ignored by the U.S. A UPI story on Arafat's proposals was the featured front-page story in *The San Francisco Examiner*, and the facts were reported without prominence in the local quality press. The national press suppressed the story outright, apart from a bare mention in *The Washington Post* some weeks later. *The New York Times* refused to publish a word and even banned letters on the topic, while continuing (along with the media in general) to denounce Arafat for his unwillingness to pursue a diplomatic course. In general, the more significant the journal, the more it was determined to suppress the facts, which is an entirely natural stance given the position of the U.S. government on the issues.[58]

Knowledgeable Israelis are, of course, aware of Arafat's stand. Former chief of military intelligence General (ret.) Yehoshaphat Harkabi, an Arabist and well-known hawk for many years, notes that the PLO wishes a political settlement because it knows that the alternative is terrible and will lead to total destruction... Arafat, like Hussein and the Arabs of the West Bank, is afraid that if there will not be a settlement, Israel will explode, and with it all its neighbors, including the Palestinians... [Therefore,] Arafat adopts relatively moderate positions with regard to Israel.[59]

These observations underscore several points: (1) there is a crucial political context in which terrorism must be understood, if we are to be serious about it; (2) it is the other fellow's crimes, not our own comparable or worse ones, that constitute "terrorism"—in this case, Palestinian but not Israeli or American crimes; (3) the concepts of "terrorism" and "retaliation" are used as terms of propaganda, not description. Crucially, the hysteria fanned over carefully selected acts of terrorism—those by Arabs, whether Palestinians, Lebanese Shi'ites, Libyans, Syrians, or even Iranians, who can count as Arabs for this purpose—is designed to achieve certain specific political goals. Further inquiry reinforces these conclusions.

Consider again the matter of retaliation. The first rocket attack by Shi'ites against Qiryat Shemona itself occurred in December 1985, after more than three years of a military occupation of extreme brutality that reached its peak during the Iron Fist operations under Shimon Peres in early 1985. But the occasionally reported savagery of the occupiers fails to convey anything like the full story, since it ignores the day-to-day reality; the same is true of the occasional reporting of Israeli atrocities in the occupied territories, which fails to convey the true picture of brutal degradation, repression, exploitation of cheap (including child) labour, harsh control over political and cultural life, and curtailment of economic development.

A more instructive picture is given by Julie Flint, who recounts "the story of life, and death, in one southern Lebanese village" of Shi'ites a month before the rocket attack. Kfar Roummane had been "a prosperous agricultural town of 8,000 people" near Nabatiya during the period when southern Lebanon was subjected to PLO terror, according to official history (see note 37). After what *The New York Times* called its "liberation" from PLO rule, Kfar Roummane was surrounded by "two huge fortifications built by the Israelis and their Lebanese proxy, the South Lebanon Army," from which there is constant sniping and shelling, "sometimes from dawn to dusk, sometimes only for a few hours," with many casualties, leading to the flight of six thousand people, leaving three-quarters of the "dying village" uninhabitable. There is no sign of resistance activity, and little likelihood of it among the apolitical farmers on a bare expanse of flat hillside.[60]

Was the shelling of Qiryat Shemona "terrorism" or "retaliation," even putting aside the murderous atrocities of the Peres-Rabin Iron Fist operations?

A look at the lives of the terrorists is also instructive. One was interviewed by *The Washington Post* in a five-part series on terrorism that is typically selective. Serving an eighteen-year sentence in an Israeli jail, he was chosen as "in many ways typical of terrorists now in jail from London to Kuwait."

"In his life, a personal tragedy (the death of his father in a bomb blast in Jerusalem in 1946) combined with the discovery of a system of belief (Marxism) to plunge him into a world of cold-blooded political murder." "The bomb that killed his father and more than 90 other persons was set by the Irgun Zionist underground group, led by Menachem Begin, at British military headquarters in what is now the King David Hotel"—as it was then.[61] He "was introduced to Marxism, he said, by the 'reality' of conditions in Palestinian camps" in the occupied West Bank.

The "reality" of the occupied territories, not only in the camps, is quite real, and is bitter and cruel, outside of the editorial pages of the nation's press, where we can learn that the occupation was "a model of future cooperation" and an "experiment in Arab-Israeli coexistence."[62] To explain is not to justify, but plainly some questions arise about the easy use of such terms as "retaliation."

Or consider Suleiman Khater, the Egyptian soldier who murdered seven Israeli tourists on a Sinai beach on October 5, 1985. The Egyptian press reported that his mother said she was "happy that these Jews had died" and a doctor in his village of Baher al-Bakr described the shootings as a warning against the "illusory peace" between Egypt and Israel. Why this shocking reaction to an unspeakable crime? The Tunis bombing a few days earlier might suggest a reason, but there may be others.

In 1970, Israeli warplanes bombed Baher al-Bakr, killing forty-seven schoolchildren, during the "war of attrition," when extensive Israeli bombing, some of it deep inside Egypt, drove a million and a half civilians from the Suez Canal area, threatening general war when Soviet-piloted MIGs defending inner Egypt were shot down by newly-acquired Israeli Phantom jets over Egyptian territory.[63]

Something is missing, then, when the *Times* Israel correspondent blandly reports that Khater "acted out of motives that were nationalist and anti-Israel"[64]—something that would surely not have been ignored had the situation been reversed.

David Hirst observes that "the main, or the really significant center of international terrorism [in the sanitised Western sense of the term] is Lebanon. It either breeds its own terrorists, or serves as a congenial home for imported ones," either Palestinians, who "have known little but bombardment, murder, massacre and mutilation, encircling hatred, fear and insecurity," or Lebanese, whose society was given its final blow by the U.S.-backed Israeli aggression and its aftermath. Among these groups,

> one conviction is rooted in the minds of the youth of today... that under President Reagan, who has carried his country's traditional partisanship with Israel to unprecedented lengths, the U.S. is the incorrigible upholder of a whole existing order so intolerable that any means now justifies its destruction. The terrorist impulse may be strongest among the Palestinians, but it can also be Lebanese, Arab, or—in its most spectacular manifestation—Shi'ite.

The essential point was expressed by Yehoshaphat Harkabi: "To offer an honorable solution to the Palestinians respecting their right to self-determination: that is the solution of the problem of terrorism. When the swamp disappears, there will be no more mosquitos."[65]

U.S.-Israeli wholesale terrorism and aggression have surely contributed to the situation Hirst describes, predictably and perhaps consciously so (see above), and both terrorist states are more than pleased at the outcome. It provides them with justification in persisting in their course of rejectionism and violence. Furthermore, the retail terrorism to which they have contributed so effectively can be exploited to induce a proper sense of fear and mobilisation among the population, as required for more general ends. All that is neceessary is a propaganda system that can be relied upon to shriek in chorus on command and to suppress any understanding of U.S. initiatives, their pattern, their sources, and their motivation. On this score, policy-makers need have few concerns.

Terrorist acts are characteristically described by their perpetrators as "retaliatory" (or, in the case of U.S. and Israeli terrorism, as "pre-emptive"). Thus the bombing of Tunis was retaliation for the murders in Larnaca, as noted, though there was barely a pretense that the victims of the Tunis bombing had any connection with the Larnaca atrocity. The latter was also justified as "retaliatory," a response to Israeli hijacking of ships travelling from Cyprus to Lebanon.[66] The former claim was accepted in the U.S. as legitimate, the latter ignored or derided, a distinction based on ideological commitment, as is the norm.

Putting aside the justification offered for terrorist violence and keeping to the factual record, there is no doubt that Israel *has* been carrying out hijacking operations and kidnapping at sea for many years. There is little notice and no concern in the U.S. over this crime, yet such actions arouse great passion and anger when the perpetrators are Arabs. It was not even deemed appropriate to report the fact that the Israeli High Court in effect gave its stamp of approval to this procedure. In the case of an Arab who appealed his imprisonment on the grounds that he was captured outside Israeli territorial waters, the High Court ruled that "the legality of sentencing and imprisonment is unaffected by the means whereby the suspect was brought to Israeli territory" and held (once again) that an Israeli court may sentence a person for actions outside of Israel that it regards as criminal. In this case, the court stated that "security reasons" made it necessary to keep the appellant in prison.[67]

Turning to the historical record, in 1976, according to Knesset Member General (ret.) Mattityahu Peled, the Israeli Navy began to capture boats belonging to Lebanese Muslims, turning them over to Israel's Lebanese Christian allies, who killed them, in an effort to abort steps towards conciliation that had been arranged between the PLO and Israel. Prime Minister Rabin conceded the facts but said that the boats were captured prior to these arrangements, while Defense Minister Shimon Peres refused to comment. After a prisoner exchange in November 1983, a front-page story in *The Times* mentioned in its eighteenth paragraph that thirty-seven of the Arab prisoners, who had been held at the notorious Ansar prison camp, "had been seized recently by the Israeli Navy as they tried to make their way from Cyprus to Tripoli," north of Beirut, an observation that merited no comment there or elsewhere.[68]

In June 1984, Israel hijacked a ferryboat operating between Cyprus and Lebanon five miles off the Lebanese coast with a burst of machine gun fire and forced it to Haifa, where nine people, eight Lebanese and one Syrian, were removed and held. Five were freed after interrogation and four were detained, including one woman and a schoolboy returning from England for a holiday in Beirut; two were released two weeks later, while the fate of the others remains unreported. The matter was considered so insignificant that one has to search for tiny items in the back pages even to learn this much about the fate of the kidnapped passengers.

The London *Observer* suggested a "political motive": to compel passengers to use the ferry operating from the Maronite port of Jounieh instead of Muslim West Beirut or to signal to the Lebanese that they are "powerless" and must come to terms with Israel.

Lebanon denounced this "act of piracy," which Godfrey Jansen described as "another item" in Israel's "long list of international thuggery."

"To maintain the maritime terrorist fiction," Jansen added, "the Israelis then bombed and bombarded a small island off

Tripoli which was said to be a base for PLO seaborne operations," a claim that he dismisses as "absurd." The Lebanese police reported that fifteen people were killed, twenty were wounded, and twenty were missing, all Lebanese, fishermen and children at a Sunni boy scout camp which was the "worst hit" target.[69]

In its report on the Israeli "interception" (to translate from Newspeak: hijacking) of the ferry, *The Times* observes that prior to the 1982 war, "the Israeli Navy regularly intercepted ships bound for or leaving the ports of Tyre and Sidon in the south and searched them for guerrillas," as usual accepting Israeli claims at face value; Syrian "interception" of civilian Israeli ships on a similar pretext might be regarded a bit differently. Similarly, Israel's hijacking of a Libyan civilian jet on February 4, 1986, was accepted with equanimity—criticised, if at all, as an error based on faulty intelligence.[70] On April 25, 1985, several Palestinians were kidnapped from civilian boats operating between Lebanon and Cyprus and sent to secret destinations in Israel, a fact that became public knowledge (in Israel) when one of the Palestinians was interviewed on Israeli television, leading to an appeal to the High Court of Justice for information; presumably there are others, unknown.[71]

None of these cases, most of which are known only through incidental comment, arouses any interest or concern, any more than when it is reported in passing that Arab "security prisoners" released in an exchange with Syria were in fact "Druze residents of villages in the Israeli-annexed portion of the strategic Golan Heights."[72] It is considered Israel's prerogative to hijack ships and to kidnap, at will, and to bombard what it will call "terrorist targets," with the approval of articulate opinion in the United States, whatever the facts may be.

We might tarry a moment over the Israeli attack on the island off Tripoli north of Beirut, in which Lebanese fishermen and boy scouts were killed. This received scant notice, but that is the norm in the case of such regular Israeli terrorist atrocities, of which this is far from the most serious.

Palestinian attacks fare differently. None is remembered with more horror than the atrocity at Ma'alot in 1974, where

79

twenty-two members of a paramilitary youth group were killed in an exchange of fire after Moshe Dayan had refused, over the objections of General Mordechai Gur, to consider negotiations on the terrorists' demands for the release of Palestinian prisoners.[73] One might ask why the murder of Lebanese boy scouts is a lesser atrocity—in fact, not an atrocity at all, since it was perpetrated by "a country that cares for human life" (*The Washington Post*) with a "high moral purpose" (*Time*) perhaps unique in history.[74]

Two days before the Ma'alot attack, Israeli jets had bombed the Lebanese village of El-Kfeir, killing four civilians. According to Edward Said, the Ma'alot attack was "preceded by weeks of sustained Israeli napalm bombing of Palestinian refugee camps in southern Lebanon" that killed more than two hundred people. At the time, Israel was engaged in large-scale scorched earth operations in southern Lebanon, with air, artillery, and gunboat attacks and commando operations using shells, bombs, anti-personnel weapons, and napalm, killing probably thousands (the West could not be troubled, so no accurate figures are available in the U.S.) and driving hundreds of thousands north to slums around Beirut.[75]

Interst was slight and reporting scanty. None of this is recorded in the annals of terrorism; nor did it even happen, as far as sanitised history is concerned, though the murderous Palestinian terrorist attacks of the early 1970s were (rightly, of course) bitterly condemned, and still stand as proof that the Palestinians cannot be a partner to negotiations over their fate.

Meanwhile, the media are regularly condemned as overly critical of Israel and even "pro-PLO," a propaganda coup of quite monumental proportions.

We might note the interpretation of these events offered by Israeli leaders honoured in the United States as "moderates"—for example, Yitzhak Rabin, who was ambassador to Washington and then prime minister during the period of the worst Israeli atrocities in Lebanon, pre-Camp David: "We could not ignore the plight of the civil population in southern Lebanon.... It was our humanitarian duty to aid the population of the area and prevent it from being wiped out by the hostile terrorists."[76] Reviewers of Rabin's memoirs, where these words appear, found nothing amiss in them, so effectively has an ideologically serviceable history been constructed, and so profound is anti-Arab racism in the West.

It should also be noted that Israel is not alone in enjoying the right of piracy and hijacking. A Tass report condemning the *Achille Lauro* hijacking in October 1985 accused the United States of hypocrisy because two men who hijacked a Soviet airliner, killing a stewardess and wounding other crew members, were given refuge in the U.S., which refused extradition.[77] The case is not exactly well known, and the charge of hypocrisy might appear to have a certain merit.

Neither is this case unique. Observes Abraham Sofaer, legal adviser to the State Department:

> During the 1950s, despite America's strong opposition to aircraft hijackings, the United States and its Western allies refused requests from Czechoslovakia, the USSR, Poland, Yugoslavia, and other communist regimes for the return of persons who hijacked planes, trains and ships to escape.

Sofaer claims that the U.S. "re-examined its policy" in the late 1960s and early 1970s "when aircraft hijacking reached epidemic proportions" and was posing "too serious a problem and too great a threat to the safety of innocent passengers to be tolerated."[78] This is Newspeak for the fact that hijacking began to be directed against the U.S. and its allies and thus fell under the category of terrorism instead of heroic resistance to oppression. Again, U.S. support for properly targeted hijacking is not prominently displayed in the media or in the productions of the rising stars of terrorology.

One might also mention the first airplane hijacking in the Middle East, which is also not familiar fare. It was carried out by Israel in December 1954, when a Syrian Airways civilian jet was intercepted by Israeli fighters and forced to land at Lydda airport. Chief-of-Staff Moshe Dayan's intent was "to get hostages in order to obtain the release of our prisoners in Damascus," Prime Minister Moshe Sharett wrote in his personal diary. The prisoners in question were Israeli soldiers who had been captured on a spy mission inside Syria. It was Dayan, we recall, who, twenty years later, ordered the rescue attempt that led to the death of Israeli teenagers in Ma'alot who had been taken hostage in an effort to obtain the release of Palestinian prisoners in Israel.

Sharett wrote privately that "we had no justification whatsoever to seize the plane" and that he had "no reason to doubt the truth of the factual affirmation of the U.S. State Department that our action was without precedent in the history of international practice." But the incident has disappeared from history, so that Israeli U.N. Ambassador Benjamin Netanyahu, now a much-admired commentator on international terrorism, may appear on national television and, with no fear of contradiction, accuse the PLO of "inventing" the hijacking of airplanes and even the killing of diplomats.[79]

As for the killing of diplomats, we might only recall the assassination of U.N. mediator Folke Bernadotte in 1948 by a terrorist group led by Netanyahu's immediate superior, Foreign Minister Yitzhak Shamir, who was one of the three commanders who gave the orders for the assassination (a second, who is now dead, was a respected commentator in the Israeli press for many years, as is the third). A close friend of David Ben-Gurion privately confessed that he was one of the assassins, but Ben-Gurion kept it secret, and the Israeli government arranged for the escape from prison and departure from the country of those responsible.

In his eyewitness account, Zionist historian Jon Kimche writes that "there was no nation-wide outcry or determination to catch the perpetrators" and "not much moral indignation." "The attitude of the majority was that another enemy of the Jews had fallen by the wayside." The assassination "was condemned, regretted and deplored because it would cast reflections on Israel, and make the work of her diplomats more difficult; not because it was wrong in itself to resort to assassination."[80]

In our conveniently selective memory, only Arab actions remain as "the evil scourge of terrorism."

After the hijacking of the *Achille Lauro* in retaliation for the Tunis bombing, the issue of ship hijacking became a major Western concern. A study by Reuters news agency concluded that "there have been just a handful of ship hijackings since 1961,"giving a few examples by Muslims; the Israeli hijackings were plainly not on the list.[81]

Hijacking is not the only form of terrorism that escapes this category when it is carried out by friends of the United States. Jeane Kirkpatrick explained that the blowing up of the Greenpeace antinuclear protest ship *Rainbow Warrior* by French agents, with one man murdered, was not terrorism: "I'd like to say that the French clearly did not intend to attack civilians and bystanders and maim, torture or kill."

In its lead editorial, under the title "Mitterrand's Finest Hour," *The Asian Wall St. Journal* wrote: "The Greenpeace campaign is fundamentally violent and dangerous... That the French government was prepared to use force against the Rainbow Warrior... suggests that the government had its priorities straight."

In *The New York Times*, David Housego reviews a book on the affair, criticising the French for "blunders" and "a bad mistake"; "there was no need" to blow up the ship and the French could have "gained the same objective with far less unfavourable publicity." There is no hint that harsher words might be in order. Given these "blunders," Housego concludes that "it was difficult to justify not incriminating [Defense Minister] Mr. Hernu and hard to blame the New Zealanders for imprisoning the French officers."[82] Housego discusses the comparison with Watergate, missing the major analogy: in that case, too, there was a great hullabaloo about "blunders" and petty criminality, and much self-congratulation on the part of the media, while both Congress and the media ignored as irrelevant the real crimes of the Nixon Administration.[83]

The emperor is exempt from the charge of terrorism and other crimes, and his allies often share the same privilege. They are guilty at worst of "blunders."

George Shultz may well deserve the prize for hypocrisy on this score. While urging an "active" drive on terrorism, he described as "insidious" the claim that "one man's terrorist is another man's freedom fighter":

> Freedom fighters or revolutionaries don't blow up buses containing non-combatants. Terrorist murderers do. Freedom fighters don't assassinate innocent businessmen or hijack innocent men, women and children. Terrorist murderers do... The resistance fighters in Afghanistan do not destroy villages or kill the helpless. The contras in Nicaragua do not blow up school buses or hold mass executions of civilians.

In fact, the terrorists Shultz commands in Nicaragua, as he knows, specialise precisely in murderous attacks on civilians, and in torture, rape, mutilation; their odious record of terror is well documented, though ignored and quickly forgotten, even denied by terrorist apologists (see note 17). The resistance fighters in Afghanistan have also carried out brutal atrocities of a sort that would evoke fevered denunciations in the West if the attacking forces (who would then be called "liberators" acting in "self-defense") were American or Israeli.

Only a few months before he spoke, Shultz's UNITA friends in Angola were boasting of having shot down civilian airliners with 266 people killed and had released twenty-six hostages who had been held as long as nine months, including twenty-one Portuguese, Spanish, and Latin American missionaries; they had also announced "a new campaign of urban terror," AP reported, noting a bombing in Luanda in which thirty people were killed and more than seventy injured when a jeep loaded with dynamite exploded in the city. They had also captured European teachers, doctors, and others—some 140 foreigners, the press reported, including sixteen British technicians "taken hostage," Jonas Savimbi stated, and not to be released until Prime Minister Thatcher offers his organisation "some kind of recognition." Such actions continue regularly: e.g., the blowing up of a hotel in April 1986, killing seven foreign civilians and wounding many others.

Savimbi "is one of the few authentic heroes of our times," Jeane Kirkpatrick declaimed at a Conservative Political Action

84

convention where Savimbi "received enthusiastic applause after vowing to attack American oil installations in his country." This plan to kill Americans did not prompt the U.S. to invoke the doctrine of "self-defense against future attack" employed to justify the bombing of "mad dog" Qaddafi, just as there was no bombing of Johannesburg when South African mercenaries were captured in May 1985 in northern Angola on a mission to destroy these facilities and kill Americans; a terrorist state must exercise subtle judgements.[84]

In the real world, Savimbi qualifies as a freedom fighter for Shultz, Kirkpatrick, and other leading terrorist commanders and advocates, primarily because "UNITA is the most extensively backed of South Africa's client groups used to destabilise the neighbouring states."[85]

As for Shultz's *contra* armies, their prime task is to hold the entire civilian population of Nicaragua hostage under the threat of sadistic terror to compel the government to abandon any commitment to the needs of the poor majority, in preference to the "moderate" and "democratic" policy of addressing the transcendent needs of U.S. business and its local associates as in more properly behaved states under the U.S. aegis.

But in the corrupt and depraved cultural climate in which these terrorist commanders and apologists thrive, Shultz's statements and others like them pass with barely a raised eyebrow.

The taking of hostages plainly falls under the rubric of terrorism. There is no doubt, then, that Israel was guilty of a serious act of international terrorism when it removed some twelve hundred prisoners, mainly Lebanese Shi'ites, and brought them to Israel in violation of international law in the course of its retreat from Lebanon. They would be released, it was explained, "on an unspecific schedule to be determined by the security situation in southern Lebanon"—making it quite clear that they were to be held hostage pending a demonstration of "good behaviour" on the part of the local population kept under guard by Israeli forces and their mercenaries in the "security zone" in southern Lebanon and in surrounding areas.

85

As Mary McGrory observed in a rare departure from the general conformity, the prisoners were "hostages in Israeli jails." "They are not criminals; they were scooped up as insurance against attack when the Israelis were finally quitting Lebanon"—in fact, there was no intention to quit southern Lebanon, where Israel retains its "security zone," and even the partial withdrawal was the achievement of the Lebanese resistance.

One hundred and forty prisoners had been secretly moved to Israel in November 1983 in violation of an agreement with the Red Cross to release them in a prisoner exchange, after the closing (temporary, as it turned out) of the Ansar prison camp, the scene of brutal atrocities, frequently described as a "concentration camp" by Israelis who served or visited there and were sickened by the barbarous behaviour of the captors; the prisoners were refused even Red Cross visits until July 1984. Israeli defense ministry spokesman Nachman Shai stated that 400 of the 766 still in custody in June 1985 had been arrested for "terrorist activities"—meaning resistance to the Israeli military occupation—while "the rest were arrested for less violent forms of political activism or organizing activities designed to undermine the Israeli Army presence in Lebanon."[86]

Israel had promised to release 340 of the hostages on June 10, "but canceled the release at the last minute for security reasons that were never fully explained."[87] Four days later, Lebanese Shi'ites, reported to be friends and relatives of the Israeli-held hostages,[88] hijacked TWA flight 847, taking hostages in an attempt to free the hostages held by Israel.

This evoked another bout of well orchestrated and utterly hypocritical hysteria in the United States, with overt racist undertones and numerous attacks on the media for allowing the hijackers an occasional opportunity to explain their position, thus interfering with the totalitarian discipline deemed appropriate within the propaganda system. The Israeli kidnappers needed no special access to the U.S. media, which were delighted to deliver their message for them, often as "news."

The media are commonly condemned for "supporting terrorism" by allowing terrorists to express their position;

the reference is not to the regular appearance of Ronald Reagan, George Shultz, Elliott Abrams, and other leading terrorists, who present their messages without any rebuttal or comment, providing the framework of concepts and assumptions for what is called "news reporting."

The press dismissed the hijackers' statements that they wished to secure the release of the Israeli-held hostages—who were, of course, not hostages in U.S. parlance, since they were held by "our side."

The absurdity of the Shi'ite pretense was easily exposed. Flora Lewis explained that "it is out of character for militant Shiites, who extol martyrdom and show little reluctance to take the lives of others, to be so concerned with the timing of the prisoners' return"—another version of the useful concept that the lower orders feel no pain.

The Times editors offered the pathetic argument that "Israel had planned to appease the resentful Shiites last week [that is, a few days prior to the TWA hijacking], but was delayed by the kidnapping of some Finnish U.N. troops in Lebanon"; in a ninety-word news item, *The Times* had noted the charge by Finland that during this entirely unrelated event "Israeli officers had watched Lebanese militiamen beat up kidnapped Finnish soldiers serving with the United Nations in Lebanon, but had done nothing to help them" while they were "beaten with iron bars, water hoses and rifles by members of the South Lebanon Army." "There are crimes aplenty here," *The Times* thundered, denouncing the TWA hijackers, the Greek authorities (for their laxity), and even the United States—for "having failed to punish Iran for sheltering the killers of two Americans in a hijacking last year" (see note 77). But the Israeli hostage-taking was not one of these crimes.[89]

Princeton Middle East historian Bernard Lewis, his scholarly reputation rendering evidence or refutation of explicit counter-evidence unnecessary, asserted unequivocally that

> the hijackers or those who sent them must have known perfectly well that the Israelis were already planning to release the Shi'ite and other Lebanese captives, and that a public challenge of this kind could only delay, rather than accelerate, their release.

87

They could proceed "to challenge America, to humiliate Americans" because they knew that the supine media would "provide them with unlimited publicity and perhaps even some form of advocacy." Recall that this is the voice of a respected scholar in a respected journal, a fact that once again yields some insight into the comical frenzy that passes for intellectual life.

The editors of *The New Republic* dismissed the Shi'ite plea for release of the Israeli-held hostages as "perfect rubbish": "Hijacking, kidnapping, murder, and massacre are the way Shiites and other factions in Lebanon do their political business," and "everyone knew" that the Israeli-held prisoners were scheduled for release—when Israel was good and ready. President Reagan escalated the hysteria yet another notch, explaining that the "real goal" of the terrorists is "to expel America from the world," no less. Norman Podhoretz, noting that use of force would probably have led to the death of American hostages, denounced Reagan for failing "to risk life itself [namely, the lives of others] in defense of the national honor." New York Mayor Edward Koch called for the bombing of Lebanon and Iran, and others struck appropriate heroic poses.[90]

Meanwhile, the careful reader could discover buried in news reports on the hostage crisis the fact that two thousand Lebanese Shi'ites, including seven hundred children, fled their homes under shelling by Israel's South Lebanon Army, who also shot at jeeps of the U.N. peace-keeping forces, while "a combined force of Israeli troops and Christian-led militiamen swept into a south Lebanese village today and seized 19 Shiite men, a United Nations spokesman announced."[91]

After the hijacking, Israel began to release its hostages according to its own timetable, which was very likely accelerated because the TWA hijacking had focused international attention on its own vastly more significant kidnapping operation. When three hundred were released on July 3, AP reported their testimony that they were tortured and starved. Thomas Friedman of *The Times*, however, heard only that "we were treated well by the Israelis...." And finally, Reagan wrote a letter to Shimon Peres "saying that the Beirut hostage crisis has strengthened relations between their countries"; nothing was said about the other "hostage crisis," which is not part of official history.[92]

Even by the standards of Western Newspeak, the Israeli actions would qualify as hostage-taking were it not for the fact that as a client of the emperor who molests the world, Israel is exempt from this charge. But it is important to stress the limits of the Orwellian concepts of contemporary political discourse, in which such terms as "terrorism" and "hostage" are construed to exclude the most extreme examples, such as Nicaragua and southern Lebanon, where entire populations are held hostage to ensure obedience to the foreign master. Such usage is obligatory, given the true nature of wholesale international terrorism and the obvious necessity to prevent any comprehension of it.

Keeping just to the Middle East, we should recognise that at some level the matter is well understood by the organisers of international terrorism.

The reason for the savage attack on southern Lebanon throughout the 1970s was explained by the Israeli diplomat Abba Eban, considered a leading dove: "There was a rational prospect, ultimately fulfilled, that affected populations would exert pressure for the cessation of hostilities." Translation: the population of southern Lebanon was being held hostage to make them compel the Palestinians to accept the status assigned to them by the Labour government represented by Eban, who had declared that the Palestinians "have no role to play" in any peace settlement.[93]

Chief of Staff Mordechai Gur explained in 1978 that "for 30 years... we have been fighting against a population that lives in villages and cities," noting such incidents as the bombing of the Jordanian city of Irbid and the expulsion by bombing of tens of thousands of inhabitants of the Jordan Valley and a million and a half civilians from the Suez Canal. These examples and others were all part of the programme of holding civilian populations hostage in an effort to prevent resistance to the political settlement that Israel imposed by force, and then proceeded to maintain, while rejecting the possibility of political settlement such as Sadat's offer of a full peace treaty on the internationally recognised borders in 1971.

Israel's regular practice of "retaliation" against defenseless civilian targets unrelated to the source of terrorist acts (themselves, often retaliation for earlier Israeli terrorism, etc.) also reflects the same conception, a departure, by the early 1950s, from Ben-Gurion's earlier dictum that "reaction is inefficient" unless it is precisely focused: "If we know the family—[we must] strike mercilessly, women and children included."[94]

Gur's understanding of Israel's wars is widely shared among the military command. During the Iron Fist operations of early 1985, Defense Minister Yitzhak Rabin warned that Israel would, if necessary, conduct "a policy of scorched earth as was the case in the Jordan Valley during the war of attrition" with Egypt. "Lebanon is a more serious source of terror than it was in 1982," he added, with Shi'ite terrorists now holding Western Europe in fear (they did not do so prior to the Israeli invasion of 1982, for unexplained reasons), so that Israel must maintain a zone in the south in which "we may intervene."

The veteran paratroop commander Dubik Tamari, who gave the orders to level the Palestinian camp of Ain el-Hilweh by air and artillery bombardment "to save lives" of troops under his command (another notable exercise of the fabled "purity of arms"), justified the action with the comment that "the State of Israel has been killing civilians from 1947," "purposely killing civilians" as "one goal among others."[95]

Tamari cited as an example the attack on Qibya in 1953, when Ariel Sharon's Unit 101 killed seventy Arab villagers in their homes in alleged retaliation for a terrorist attack with which they had no connection whatsoever. Ben-Gurion pretended on Israeli radio that the villagers were killed by Israeli civilians enraged by Arab terror, "mostly refugees, people from Arab countries and survivors from the Nazi concentration camps," dismissing the "fantastic allegation" that Israeli military forces were involved—a brazen lie which, furthermore, placed Israeli settlements under threat of retaliation for this cold-blooded massacre.

Less known is the fact that a month before the Qibya massacre, Moshe Dayan had sent Unit 101 to drive four thousand Beduins of the Azzazma and Tarbin tribes across the Egyptian border—another step in expulsions that had been proceeding from 1950, shortly after the ceasefire. In March 1954, eleven Israelis were murdered in an ambush of a bus in the Eastern Negev by members of the Azzazma tribe ("unprovoked terrorism"), evoking an Israeli raid on the completely unrelated Jordanian village of Nahaleen with nine villagers killed ("retaliation"). In August 1953, Sharon's Unit 101 had killed twenty people, two-thirds of them women and children, at the al-Bureig refugee camp in the Gaza Strip, in "retaliation" for infiltration.[96]

The cycle of "retaliation" (by Jews) and "terror" (by Palestinians) can be traced back, step-by-step, for many years, an exercise that will quickly reveal that the terminology belongs to the realm of propaganda, not description.

Here, too, we might note how effectively history has been reconstructed in a more ideologically serviceable form. Thus, Thomas Friedman, reviewing "Israel's counter-terrorism" strategy, writes that "the first period, from 1948 to 1956, might best be described as the era of counterterrorism-through-retaliation, or negative feedback," though "at least one of these retaliations became highly controversial, involving civilian casualties," the reference presumably being to Qibya. The record of scholarship is often hardly different.[97]

The Iron Fist operations of the Israeli army in southern Lebanon in early 1985 were also guided by the logic outlined by Eban, as already discussed. The civilian population was held hostage under the threat of terror to ensure that it accept the political arrangements dictated by Israel in southern Lebanon and the occupied territories. The warnings remain in effect; the population is still held hostage, with no concern in the superpower that finances these operations and bars any meaningful political settlement.

While wholesale terrorism, including the holding of hostages, is exempt from censure in Western Newspeak when conducted by an approved source, the same is true of smaller-scale operations, as already illustrated. To mention a few other characteristic cases, in November-December 1983, Israel "made it clear that it would not allow Arafat's forces to evacuate the city [Tripoli, in northern Lebanon, where they were under attack by Syrian-backed forces] as long as the fate of the Israeli prisoners was in doubt." Israel therefore bombed what were called "guerrilla positions," preventing the departure of Greek ships that were to evacuate Arafat loyalists. Druze spokesmen reported that a hospital was hit during the bombing and strafing of "what were described as Palestinian bases," east of Beirut, while in Tripoli, "one already-gutted cargo ship took a direct hit and sank" and "a freighter burst into flames when it was hit."[98] Again, the population was held hostage, as were foreign vessels, to ensure the release of Israeli prisoners captured in the course of Israel's aggression in Lebanon. There was no comment in the United States on this further atrocity, as usual.

In Lebanon and the Mediterranean Sea, Israel carries out attacks with utter impunity and abandon.

In mid-July 1985, Israeli warplanes bombed and strafed Palestinian camps near Tripoli, killing at least twenty people, most of them civilians, including six children under twelve. "Clouds of smoke and dust engulfed the Tripoli refugee camps, home to more than 25,000 Palestinians, for several hours after the 2:55 p.m. attack," which was assumed to be "retaliation" for two car-bomb attacks a few days earlier in Israel's "security zone" in southern Lebanon by a group aligned with Syria. Two weeks later, Israeli gunboats attacked a Honduran-registered cargo ship a mile from the port of Sidon, delivering cement, according to its Greek captain, setting it ablaze with thirty shells and wounding civilians in subsequent shore bombardment when militiamen returned the fire.

The mainstream press did not even bother to report that the following day Israeli gunboats sank a fishing boat and damaged three others, while a Sidon parliamentarian called on the U.N. to end U.S.-backed Israeli "piracy."

The press did report what Israel called a "surgical" operation against "terrorist installations" near Baalbek in the Bekaa Valley in January 1984, killing about one hundred people, mostly civilians, and wounding four hundred, including 150 children in a bombed-out schoolhouse. The "terrorist installations" also included a mosque, a hotel, a restaurant, stores, and other buildings in the three Lebanese villages and Palestinian refugee camp that were attacked, while Beirut news reported that a cattle market and an industrial park were also struck with scores of houses destroyed. A Reuters reporter in the bombed villages said that a second round of bombing began ten minutes after the first, "adding to the number of those killed or wounded" since men and women had begun dragging the dead and wounded from the wrecked buildings. He saw "lots of children" in hospitals, while witnesses reported men and women rushing to schools in a frantic search for their children.

The leader of Lebanon's Shi'ites denounced "Israeli barbarism," describing the attacks on "innocent civilians, hospitals and houses of worship" as an attempt "to terrorize the Lebanese peoople." But the incident passed without comment in the United States, in no way affecting Israel's status as "a country that cares for human life" (*The Washington Post*), so we may conclude again that the victims of this surgical bombing were less than human, as indeed they are within the racist Western consensus.[99]

One may, again, imagine what the reaction would be in the West, including the "pro-Arab" media, if the PLO or Syria were to carry out a "surgical strike" against "terrorist installations" near Tel Aviv, killing one hundred civilians and wounding four hundred others, including 150 children in a bombed-out schoolhouse, along with other civilian targets.

The standard version in the United States is that Israeli violence, although perhaps excessive at times, is "retaliation" for Arab atrocities. Israel, like the United States, claims much broader rights: the right to carry out terrorist attacks to prevent potential actions against it, as in the justification for the Lebanon war by the dovish Knesset Member Amnon Rubinstein, cited earlier.

Israeli troops carry out what they call "preventive gunfire" as they patrol in Lebanon, spraying the terrain with machine gun fire, leading Irish peace-keeping forces to block the road in protest. Quite commonly, Israeli attacks in Lebanon were described as "preventive, not punitive," the bombing and strafing of Palestinian refugee camps and nearby villages by thirty Israeli jets on December 2, 1975, for example, killing fifty-seven people. This was apparently retaliation for the decision of the U.N. Security Council to debate an Arab peace proposal to which Israel violently objected and which therefore has been excised from history.[100]

When Israeli airborne and amphibious forces attacked Tripoli in northern Lebanon in February 1973, killing thirty-one people (mainly civilians), according to Lebanese authorities, and destroying classrooms, clinics, and other buildings, Israel justified the raid as "intended to forestall a number of planned terrorist attacks against Israelis overseas."[101]

The pattern is regular, and the justifications are accepted in the United States as legitimate, again reflecting the status of Israel as a useful client state and the subhuman status of its victims.

The last case mentioned occurred on the day that Israel shot down a Libyan civilian airliner lost in a sandstorm two minutes flight time from Cairo, towards which it was heading, with 110 people killed. The U.S. officially expressed its sympathy to the families of those involved, but the press spokesman "declined to discuss with reporters the Administration's feelings about the incident." Israel blamed the French pilot, with *The Times* dutifully in tow, accepting the Israeli claim that the pilot knew he had been ordered to land but instead resorted to "highly suspicious" evasive action—the justification offered by the USSR for downing KAL 007[102]—so that the Israeli act was "at worst... an act of callousness that not even the savagery of previous Arab actions can excuse."

The official Israeli reaction came from Prime Minister Golda Meir: "The government of Israel expresses its deep sorrow for the loss of human life and is sorry that the Libyan [*sic*] pilot did not respond to the warnings given him in accordance with international practice." Shimon Peres added that "Israel acted in accordance with international laws." Israel falsely claimed that the pilot was not authorised to fly the jet plane.

"The press was forbidden to publish pictures of the destroyed plane, of the dead and the wounded," Amiram Cohen observes in a detailed analysis of the Israeli reaction (undertaken after the KAL 007 atrocity), and "journalists were not allowed

94

to visit the hospital in Beersheba and to interview survivors," all part of a "disinformation" effort.

The international reaction was dismissed by the Israeli press as yet another demonstration of the fact that "the spirit of anti-Semitism flourishes" in Europe, which is virtually a reflex response, in the U.S. as well, when someone dares mention or criticise an Israeli atrocity.

The Israeli press insisted that "Israel is not responsible"and that "one must blame the [French] pilot." It was "a mobilized press," firm in support of Israel's actions, Cohen observes. After numerous lies, Israel confirmed that there had been an "error of judgement" and agreed to make *ex gratia* payments to the families of victims "in deference to humanitarian considerations" while denying any "guilt" or Israeli responsibility.[103]

The incident was passed over quickly in the United States, with little criticism of the perpetrators of the crime. Prime Minister Golda Meir arrived in the U.S. four days later; she was troubled by few embarrassing questions by the press and returned home with new gifts of military aircraft. As noted earlier, the reaction was slightly different when the Russians shot down KAL 007 in September 1983,[104] though it was comparable when our UNITA friends claimed to have shot down two civilian airliners at the same time. It is not difficult to discern the criteria for "international terrorism."

The record of Israeli terrorism goes back to the origins of the state—indeed, long before that: the massacre of 250 civilians and the brutal expulsion of seventy thousand others from Lydda and Ramle in July 1948; the massacre of hundreds at the undefended village of Doueimah near Hebron in October 1948 in another of the numerous "land clearing operations" conducted while the international propaganda apparatus was proclaiming, as it still does, that the Arabs were fleeing at the call of their leaders; the murder of several hundred Palestinians by the IDF after the conquest of the Gaza Strip in 1956; the slaughters in Qibya, Kafr Kassem, and a string of other assassinated villages; the expulsion of thousands of Beduins from the demilitarised zones shortly after the 1948 war and thousands more from northeastern Sinai in the early

1970s, their villages destroyed, to open the region for Jewish settlement; and on, and on.

The victims, by definition, are "PLO partisans," hence terrorists; thus the respected editor of *Ha'aretz*, Gershom Schocken, can write that Ariel Sharon "made a name for himself from the early 1950s as a ruthless fighter against Palestine Liberation Organization (PLO) partisans," referring to the slaughters of civilians he conducted at al-Bureig and Qibya in 1953 (long before the PLO existed). And the victims in Lebanon and elsewhere are also "terrorists," else they could not have been killed by a state that is so devoted to "purity of arms" and is held to a "higher law" by the "pro-Arab" American press.

The terrorist commanders are honoured. When the leading contemporary U.S. terrorist took over the presidency in 1981, Israel's prime minister and foreign minister were both notorious terrorist commanders. The highest position in the Jewish Agency was held by a man who had murdered several dozen civilians he was holding under guard in a mosque in a Lebanese town during yet another land-clearing operation in 1948, to be quickly amnestied, all trace of the crime removed from the record, and granted a lawyer's license on the grounds that "no stigma" could be attached to his act. [105]

Even terrorism against Americans is tolerable. The Israeli terrorist attacks against U.S. installations (also, public places) in Egypt in 1954, in an attempt to exacerbate U.S.-Egyptian relations and abort secret peace negotiations then in progress, were ignored at the time and are barely remembered. An attempt by Israeli bombers and torpedo boats to sink the U.S. spy ship *Liberty* in international waters in 1967, even shooting lifeboats out of the water to ensure that no one would escape, with thirty-four crewmen killed and 171 injured—the worst peacetime U.S. naval disaster of the century—was dismissed as an "error"—a transparent absurdity—and is hardly known. [106] Similarly, torture of Americans by the Israeli army in the West Bank and southern Lebanon is barely noted in the media, with Israeli denials highlighted and verification by the U.S. ambassador in Israel ignored. [107] The fact that the victims were Arab-Americans no doubt serves as justification, by media standards.

What is striking about this record, which includes ample terrorism against Jews as well from the earliest days, is that it in no way sullies Israel's American reputation for moral standards, which is unequalled in history. Each new act of terrorism, if it is noted at all, is quickly dismissed and forgotten, or described as merely a deviation from perfection, the hideous nature of the enemy forcing Israel to depart, if only for a moment, from its path of righteousness.

Meanwhile, the media are regularly denounced for their "double standard" as they ignore Arab crimes while holding Israel to impossible standards; and respected scholars—their reputations untarnished by such absurdities—inform us soberly that "numerous public figures in the West, even a number of Western governments" (naturally, all unnamed) have encouraged the PLO to destroy Israel.[108]

Across the political spectrum in the United States and among the educated classes with remarkable uniformity and only the most marginal of exceptions, the unchallenged doctrine is that it is the terrorism of the Palestinians and their Arab allies, urged on by the Kremlin, their unremitting commitment to kill Jews and destroy Israel and their refusal to consider any political settlement, that is the root cause of the endless Arab-Israeli conflict, of which Israel is the pathetic victim. As for the United States, it is powerless in the face of "the evil scourge of terrorism," from Central America to Lebanon and beyond.

The Jewish national movement and the state that developed from it have broken no new ground in their impressive record of terrorist atrocities, apart from the immunity they enjoy in enlightened Western opinion. For Americans, it suffices to recall "that Adolf Hitler chose to praise the United States... for 'solving the problem' of the native races,"[109] as do some of those who live by Hitler's code in Central America today, with U.S. support. But the recent commentary on "terrorism" in the "civilised countries" reeks of hypocrisy, and can only be an object of contempt among decent people.

Notes

1. *The New York Times*, Oct. 17, 18, 1985.
2. *Ha'aretz*, March 22, 1985; Noam Chomsky, *The Fateful Triangle: Israel, the United States, and the Palestinians* (Black Rose Books, 1984), pp. 54, 75, 202.
3. Yossi Beilin, *Mechiro shel Ichud* (Tel Aviv, 1985), p. 147; Gazit, *Hamakel Vehagezer* (Tel Aviv, 1985), quoted in *Al Hamishmar*, Nov. 7, 1985; Noam Chomsky, *Towards a New Cold War* (Pantheon, 1982), pp. 267-68.
4. When I refer to Reagan, of course, I am speaking not of the symbolic figure who holds office but of the policy-makers and propagandists of the Administration.
5. *Yediot Ahronot*, Nov. 15, 1985.
6. Ze'ev Schiff, *Ha'aretz*, Feb. 8, 1985; see *The Fateful Triangle, op. cit.*, for testimony from participants that was not reported in the U.S. and for denial of the facts by apologists for Israeli terror, on the grounds that the media are anti-Semitic and "pro-PLO" while "Arabs exaggerate" and "no onus falls on lying" in "Arab culture" (Martin Peretz; the latter insight in *The New Republic*, Aug. 29, 1983).
7. See note 48, below.
8. Godfrey Jansen, *Middle East International*, Oct. 11, 1985, citing *The Los Angeles Times*, Oct. 3.
9. It appears in *Against the Current*, Jan. 1986.
10. *The Fateful Triangle, op. cit.*, pp. 127, 176.
11. Bernard Gwertzman, *The New York Times*, Oct. 2, 7, 1985.
12. Beverly Beyette, report on the International Conference on Terrorism, *The Los Angeles Times*, April 9, 1986.
13. Edward Schumacher, *The New York Times*, Oct. 22, 1985.
14. *The New Republic*, Oct. 21, 1985, Jan. 20, 1986; AP, April 4, 1986.
15. Robert McFadden, "Terror in 1985: Brutal Attacks, Tough Response," *The New York Times*, Dec. 30, 1985.
16. UPI, *The Los Angeles Times*, Dec. 28, 1985; McFadden, *op. cit.*; Dershowitz, *The New York Times*, Oct. 17, 1985; Alexander Cockburn, *The Nation*, Nov. 2, 1985, the sole notice of the shameful hypocrisy.
17. Ross Gelbspan, *The Boston Globe*, Dec. 16, 1985. On *contra* atrocities, see the regular reports of Americas Watch and numerous other careful and detailed inquiries, among them *Report of Donald T. Fox, Esq., and Prof. Michael J. Glennon to the*

International Human Rights Law Group and the Washington Office on Latin America. April 1985. They cite a high-ranking State Department official who described the U.S. stance as one of "intentional ignorance." The extensive and horrifying record is also generally disregarded by the media and others, and even flatly denied (without a pretense of evidence) by some of the more extreme apologists for Western atrocities, e.g. Robert Conquest, "Laying Propaganda on Thick," *The Daily Telegraph* (London), April 19, 1986, who assures us that the charges by Oxfam and others are not only false but "silly." See also Gary Moore, *National Interest*, Summer 1986, with a similar message; or Jeane Kirkpatrick (*The Boston Globe*, March 16, 1986), who tells us that "the contras have a record of working hard to avoid harming civilians. They have done nothing that compares with the systematic brutality the Sandinista government visits on dissenters and opponents"; comparable lies and apologetics for Soviet atrocities would not be tolerated for a moment in the media. See also note 44. The usual procedure is not to deny but simply to ignore atrocities committed by Western proxies or clients. For comic relief, one may turn to the productions of a considerable industry devoted to fabricating claims that critics of U.S. violence reject or ignore reports of atrocities by official enemies. For some examples, including quite spectacular lies, see Noam Chomsky and Edward S. Herman, *The Political Economy of Human Rights*, Vol. II: *After the Cataclysm: Postwar Indochina and the Reconstruction of Imperial Ideology* (Black Rose Books, 1979); my "Decade of Genocide in Review," *Inside Asia* (London), Feb.-March 1985, and "Visions of Righteousness," *Cultural Critique*, Spring 1986; Christopher Hitchens, "The Chorus and Cassandra," *Grand Street*, Autumn 1985.

18. *The New York Times*, June 29, 1985.
19. And in Israel. After his accession to power, there was an increase in the use of torture in prisons, administrative detention, expulsion in violation of international law, and sealing of houses, practices that were common under the previous Labour government much lauded by left-liberal American opinion, but reduced or suspended under Menachem Begin. Danny Rubinstein, *Davar*, Feb. 4, 1986; Eti Ronel, *Al Hamishmar*, June 11, 1986. On torture, see *Ha'aretz*, Feb. 24, 1986; and Ghadda Abu Jaber, *1985—Policy of Torture Renewed*, Alternative Information Center, Jerusalem, Feb. 1986; *Koteret Rashit*, May 7, 1986. See also Amnesty International, "Town Arrest Orders in Israel and the Occupied Territories," Oct. 2, 1985.

20. Curtis Wilkie, *The Boston Globe*, March 10; Julie Flint, *The Guardian* (London), March 13; Jim Muir, *Middle East International*, March 22; Breindel, *The New York Times*. Op-Ed, March 28; Nora Boustany, *The Washington Post*, March 12, 1985. A photo of the wall graffiti appears in Joseph Schechia, *The Iron Fist* (ADC, Washington, 1985).

21. *The Guardian* (London), March 2, 6, 1985.

22. Ilya, *The Jerusalem Post*, Feb. 27, 1985; Magnus Linklater, Isabel Hilton, and Neal Ascherson, *The Fourth Reich* (Hodder & Stoughton, London, 1984), p. 111); *Der Spiegel*, April 21, 1986 (see Chapter 3); *The New York Times*, March 13, 1985.

23. Ihsan Hijazi, *The New York Times*, Jan. 1, 1986; Hijazi notes that the reports from Israel differed.

24. *The Christian Science Monitor*, Jan. 30, 1986.

25. For detailed examination of this question, see my *Fateful Triangle, op. cit.* Or compare, for example, what appeared in *Newsweek* with what bureau chief Tony Clifton describes in his book *God Cried* (Clifton and Catherine Leroy, Quartet, 1983), published in London. Or consider *My War Diary* by Col. Dov Yermiya, one of the founders of the Israeli army, published in violation of censorship in Israel (see *The Fateful Triangle* for many quotes) and later in English translation (South End, 1983), but entirely ignored in the media, though it is obviously a work of considerable importance. There are numerous other examples.

26. Landrum Bolling, ed., *Reporters Under Fire* (Westview, 1985). Included, for example, is a critique of the media by the Anti-Defamation League of B'nai Brith and other accusations which barely rise to the level of absurdity (see my *Fateful Triangle, op. cit.*, for analysis of these documents), but not a study by the American-Arab Anti-Discrimination Committee that presents evidence of "a consistent pro-Israeli bias" in press coverage of the war.

27. Kifner, *The New York Times*, March 10; Muir, *Middle East International*, Feb. 22, 1985; Mary Curtius, *The Christian Science Monitor*, March 22; Jim Yamin, *The Christian Science Monitor*, April 25; Yamin, interview, *MERIP Reports*, June 1985; David Hirst, *The Guardian* (London), April 2; Robert Fisk, *The Times* (London), April 26, 27; *The Philadelphia Inquirer*, April 28, 1985. On Israeli efforts to fuel hostilities in the Chouf region from mid-1982, see my *Fateful Triangle, op. cit.*, p. 418f.

28. *Middle East International*, March 22, 1985.

29. UPI, *The Boston Globe*, Sept. 22, 1984; Olmert, interview, *Al Hamishmar*, Jan. 27, 1984; Hirsh Goodman, *The Jerusalem*

Post, Feb. 10, 1984; Wieseltier, *The New Republic*, April 8, 1985.

30. Don Oberdorfer, "The Mind of George Shultz," *The Washington Post Weekly*, Feb. 17, 1986; Rubin, *The New Republic*, June 2, 1986; Thomas Friedman, *The New York Times*, Feb. 16, 1986, among many other reports. Like Wieseltier, Rubin asserts that this Syrian-sponsored "terrorism... is not a cry of outrage against a Western failure to pursue peace but an attempt to block diplomacy altogether," since "almost any conceivable solution is anathema to the Syrian government." Rubin knows that Syria has supported diplomatic solutions close to the international consensus, but since they are remote from U.S. rejectionism, these solutions are not "conceivable" and do not count as "diplomatic options"; see Chapter 1.

31. *The Los Angeles Times*, Oct. 18, 1985.

32. *The New York Times*, Oct. 18, 1985.

33. Ze'ev Schiff, "The Terror of Rabin and Berri," *Ha'aretz*, March 8, 1985; also General Ori Or, commander of the IDF northern command, IDF radio; FBIS, April 15, 1985.

34. Gershom Schocken, editor of *Ha'aretz*. *Foreign Affairs*, Fall 1984.

35. Shimon Peres, *The New York Times*, July 8, 1983. On the atrocities in Khiam, see my *Towards a New Cold War. op. cit.*, pp. 396-97; *The Fateful Triangle. op. cit.*, p. 191; Yoram Hamizrahi, *Davar*, June 7, 1984; press reports cited in the Democratic Front publication *Nisayon Leretsach-Am Bilvanon: 1982* (Tel Aviv, 1983). On Nabatiya, see *The Fateful Triangle*, pp. 70, 187.

36. Jim Muir, *The Sunday Times* (London), April 14, 1985; *The Christian Science Monitor*, April 15, 1985; Joel Greenberg, *The Christian Science Monitor*, Jan. 30, 1986; Sonia Dayan, Paul Kessler, and Graud de la Pradelle, *Le Monde diplomatique*, April 1986; Menahem Horowitz, *Ha'aretz*, June 30, 1986, noting the exclusion of the Red Cross, torture, etc., and observing that Israel has learned "the lesson of Ansar," the concentration camp (see below) run by the IDF, and is now permitting its SLA mercenaries to run the Khiam torture chamber so as to deflect criticism. Extensive reports of torture by former prisoners, ignored in the West, appear in *Information Bulletin 21*, 1985, International Center for Information on Palestinian and Lebanese Prisoners, Deportees, and Missing Persons, Paris. Citing this evidence, Paul Kessler (of the Collège de France, co-founder of the French Physicians Committee on Soviet Jewry) observes

that most of the prisoners "were picked up as suspects during search operations or were villagers arrested for refusing to cooperate with the occupying power, and in particular, for refusing to join the Israeli-led 'South Lebanese Army militia'." None has been indicted or tried; some had then been detained for over a year. Khiam is the principal, but not the only centre. He reports systematic torture by SLA guards, who operate the prisons "under the direction of Israeli officers" (*Israel & Palestine* (Paris), July 1986).

37. Benny Morris and David Bernstein, *The Jerusalem Post*, July 23, 1982; for comparison by Israeli journalists of life under the PLO and under Israel's Christian allies in Lebanon, a picture considerably at variance with approved doctrine in the United States, see my *Fateful Triangle, op. cit*, p. 186f. Particularly significant is the report from Lebanon by the Israeli journalist Attallah Mansour, of Maronite origin.

38. *The Economist*, Nov. 19, 1977.

39. John Cooley, in Edward Haley and Lewis Snider, eds., *Lebanon in Crisis* (Syracuse, 1979). See my *Towards a New Cold War. op. cit.*, p. 321; *The Fateful Triangle. op. cit.*, pp. 70, 84.

40. Edward Haley, *Qaddafi and the United States Since 1969* (Praeger, 1984), p. 74.

41. James Markham, *The New York Times*, Dec. 4, 1975.

42. AP, *The New York Times*, Feb. 21; Julie Flint, *The Guardian* (London), Feb. 24; Ihsan Hijazi, *The New York Times*, Feb. 28; AP, Feb. 20, 1986. The only detailed account in the U.S., to my knowledge, was by Nora Boustany, *The Washington Post*, March 1, though with the IDF role largely excised, possibly by the editors, since reporters on the scene knew well what was happening—including murder of fleeing villagers by Israeli helicopter gunships, beating and torture in the presence of Israeli officers, etc., as some have privately indicated. There is little doubt that stories were rewritten in home offices to delete mention of the IDF.

43. Ihsan Hijazi, *The New York Times*, March 25; Dan Fisher, *The Los Angeles Times*, March 28; AP, April 7; Hijazi, *The New York Times*, April 8, 1986.

44. See, for example, Robert S. Leiken, "Who Says the Contras Cannot Succeed?" *The Washington Post*, July 27, 1986—dismissing without argument the extensive record of atrocities by the terrorists he supports in the usual style of apologists (see note 17), and with the Maoist prattle about peasant armies and U.S.-USSR conflict familiar from his writings; see my articles in Walker, *op. cit.*, and Chapter 3, note 3.

45. Peres, *The New York Times*, July 8, 1983; Breindel, *op. cit.*; *The New York Times*, Sept. 16, 1983, June 3, 1985; Kamm, *The New York Times*, April 26, 1985; Friedman, *The New York Times*, Jan. 9, Feb. 20, Feb. 18, 1985; Brzezinski, *The New York Times*, Oct. 9, 1983; Reagan, press conferences, *The New York Times*, March 29, 1984, Oct. 28, 1983. See also the remarks by Rabbi Alexander Schindler, President of the Union of American Hebrew Congregations (Reform): the PLO "threatened to destroy what was left of Beirut rather than surrender"; sending the Marines to oversee their departure instead of permitting Israel to finish the job was "surely the most ignominious"assignment the Marines were ever given (UPI, *The Boston Globe*, Oct. 28, 1984). These intriguing illustrations of religion in the service of state violence are omitted from *The Times'* account that same day.

46. *The New York Times*, June 7, 1983.

47. Quandt, *American-Arab Affairs*, Fall 1985; Hillel Schenker, interview with David Shipler, *New Outlook* (Tel Aviv), May 1984.

48. The opposition Labour Party backed the war, partly because poll results indicated that ninety-eight percent of the Likud and ninety-one percent of Labour supporters regarded it as justified. As the war ended with the horrendous bombing of Beirut in mid-August, support for Begin and Sharon reached its peak of eighty-two percent and seventy-eight percent, respectively, dropping to seventy-two percent and sixty-four percent, respectively, after the Sabra-Shatila massacres. See my *Fateful Triangle, op. cit.*, pp. 251-262, 394, 378f.

49. Philip Weiss, *The New Republic*, Feb. 10, 1986.

50. Ze'ev Schiff and Ehud Ya'ari, *Israel's Lebanon War* (Simon & Schuster, 1984), p. 35; John Kifner, *The New York Times*, July 25, 1981. Schiff and Ya'ari claim that "despite the great pains taken to pinpoint the targets and achieve direct hits, over 100 people were killed," including thirty "terrorists." The Schiff-Ya'ari book is a translation of parts of the Hebrew original; about twenty percent of the original was excised by the Israeli censor according to Ya'ari (*Kol Ha'ir*, Feb. 2, 1984), about fifty percent according to the American scholar Augustus Norton, citing a "respected correspondent—unconnected to the authors" (*Middle East Journal*, Summer 1985). Censorship in Nicaragua, under attack by a U.S. proxy army, arouses great indignation in the U.S. The most extreme censorship in Israel, of course, is directed against Arabs, including Israeli

citizens. See my *Fateful Triangle. op. cit.*, p. 139f., *Turning the Tide: The U.S. and Latin America* (Black Rose Books, second revised edition, 1987), p. 73f., and my article in Walker, *op. cit.*, for a small sample.

51. Walsh, *The Washington Post Weekly*, March 4, 1985; Wilkie, *The Boston Globe*, Feb. 18, 1985.

52. *The Fateful Triangle. op. cit.*, pp. 448, 440, citing Israeli press; *News From Within* (Tel Aviv), Oct. 1, 1985; *Yediot Ahronot*, Nov. 4, 1983.

53. *Ha'aretz*, June 25, 1982; see *The Fateful Triangle. op. cit.*, p. 200f., for further quotes and similar analyses by other Israeli commentators.

54. B. Michael, *Ha'aretz*, Nov. 13, 1983; Bachar, *Yediot Ahronot*, Nov. 11, 1983; Morris, *The Jerusalem Post*, June 5, 1984.

55. *The New Republic*, ever vigilant to defend Israel from the "many press people" who are "prepared to believe just about anything reflecting badly on the Jewish state (and, almost as a corollary, anything reflecting well on its enemies)," denounced *The Washington Post* for having "collaborated in one of the great calumnies" by observing that Sharon had attempted to construct what he called "a 'new order' (the Hitler phrase)" in Lebanon (Martin Peretz, *The New Republic*, March 18, 1985; *The New Republic*, March 19, 1984). The phrase was Hitler's, and Sharon used it, as does Israeli commentary generally. One month before their condemnation of *The Post* for stating the facts accurately, a headline in the right-wing mass circulation journal *Yedioth Ahronot* read: "Sharon announced in advance his plan for 'a new order'," citing American Ambassador Morris Draper who quoted Sharon in a closed meeting of the Jewish Federation in Los Angeles (Feb. 23, 1984). The usage is standard; see my *Fateful Triangle. op. cit.*, for other examples, and for other cases where *The New Republic* carefully avoids Israeli sources in its efforts to contain deviations from the party line (e.g., pp. 215f, 258f.).

56. Olmert, *Ma'ariv*, Nov. 22, 1983; Milson, *Koteret Rashit*, Nov. 9, 1983; Sharon, cited by Ze'ev Schiff, *Ha'aretz*, May 23, 1982; Milshtein, *Hadashot*, Sept. 26, 1984; Rubinstein, *Ha'olam Haze*, June 8, 1983. On Ben-Gurion's aspirations before and after the state was established, see *The Fateful Triangle, op. cit.*, pp. 51, 160f.; Shabtai Tevet, *Ben-Gurion and the Palestinian Arabs* (Oxford, 1985) and the review by Benny Morris, *The Jerusalem Post*, Oct. 11, 1985.

57. *The Fateful Triangle, op. cit.*, p. 199, citing an interview in *Ha'aretz*, June 4, 1982; *The Fateful Triangle*, pp. 117, 263.

58. *Le Nouvel Observateur*, May 4; *The Observer* (London), April 29; *The Jerusalem Post*, May 16; *The San Francisco Examiner*, May 5; *The Washington Post*, July 8, 1984. See my "Manufacture of Consent," *Our Generation*, Vol. 17, No. 1, Sept. 1985, and my "United States and the Middle East," *END Papers* (U.K.), Summer 1985, for further details. On earlier Israeli determination to evade a political settlement, with regular U.S. support, see my *Fateful Triangle, op. cit.*, and Beilin, *op. cit.* Archival materials recently released in Israel make clear that the story goes back many years. On *New York Times* successes in creating an appropriate history, in this and other areas, see Chapter 1 and my "All the News That Fits," *UTNE Reader*, Feb.-March 1986.

59. *Ha'aretz*, Sept. 29, 1985 (cited by Amnon Kapeliouk, *Le Monde diplomatique*, Nov. 1985); *Koteret Rashit*, Oct. 9, 1985.

60. Julie Flint, *The Manchester Guardian Weekly*, Jan. 19, 1986.

61. *The Post* does not describe this as a "terrorist act" carried out by the "terrorist commander" Menachem Begin.

62. Christian Williams, Bob Woodward, and Richard Harwood, "Who Are They?" *The Washington Post*, Feb. 10, 1984; editorial, *The New York Times*, May 19, 1976. On the reality, generally suppressed in the United States, see my *Towards a New Cold War* and *Fateful Triangle, op. cit.* The behaviour of certain "human rights" organisations in this regard is noteworthy. Thus to ensure that it would have no unpleasant information, the International League for Human Rights suspended its Israeli affiliate on the sole grounds that the governing Labour Party had attempted to destroy it by measures so crude that they were quickly blocked by the Israeli courts; see my *Peace in the Middle East?* (Pantheon, 1974), pp. 196-97, *Fateful Triangle*, pp. 142, 178, and references cited. Such behaviour with regard to any other country would be regarded with utter outrage, but it does not affect the reputation of the International League. Similarly, the human rights information journal *Human Rights Internet*, which simply reports, without comment, allegations of human rights violations, permits the Anti-Defamation League to respond to charges concerning Israel, a practice excluded for any other state; thus the Communist Party, which has domestic credentials comparable to the ADL as a human rights organisation, is not given space to respond to charges against the USSR, rightly so, of course.

63. *New Outlook* (Tel Aviv), Oct. 1985; *Davar*, July 18, 1985. Military historian Uri Milshtein writes that contrary to the standard accounts, Israel initiated the conflict that led to the "war of attrition" with tank firing against Egyptian positions, killing dozens of soldiers; *Monitin*, Aug. 1984.

64. Thomas Friedman, *The New York Times*, Jan. 31, 1986.

65. Hirst, *The Manchester Guardian Weekly*, April 20, 1986; Harkabi, quoted by Amnon Kapeliouk, *Le Monde diplomatique*, Feb. 1986.

66. The PLO claimed that the three Israelis murdered had been involved in these operations, a highly implausible charge as Israeli journalist David Shaham comments (John Bulloch, "PLO victims were Mossad agents," *The Daily Telegraph* (London), Oct. 3, 1985; Shaham, *Al Fajr*, Nov. 29, 1985).

67. *Ha'aretz,* June 12, 1986. The report gives no indication that a trial took place.

68. *The Fateful Triangle, op. cit.,* p. 77; David Shipler, *The New York Times*, Nov. 25, 1983; *The New York Times*, Jan. 26, 1984, last paragraph.

69. *The New York Times*, June 30, July 1; *The Boston Globe*, July 1, 4, 12; *The Middle East Reporter* (Beirut), June 30; *The Observer* (London), July 1; Jansen, *Middle East International*, July 13, 1984.

70. Thomas Friedman, *The New York Times*, Feb. 5; the U.S. "refrained from making a judgment on the Israeli action" (*The New York Times*, Feb. 5); also Norman Kempster, *The Los Angeles Times*, Feb. 5, 1986.

71. *News From Within* (Jerusalem), Nov. 1, 1985.

72. *The Los Angeles Times, The Boston Globe*, June 29, 1984. On the severe repression in the Golan, see *The Fateful Triangle, op. cit.*, p. 132f.

73. See Uri Milshtein, *Monitin*, Aug. 1984, for a recent account.

74. See the preface.

75. *The Fateful Triangle. op. cit.*, p. 188f.

76. *The Rabin Memoirs* (Little, Brown, 1979), pp. 280-81.

77. *The New York Times*, Oct. 12, 1985. Meanwhile, *The Times* denounces Iran, "which has yet to extradite or punish those who hijacked a Kuwaiti airliner and killed two Americans in December, 1984," and demands that the West boycott Libya if Qaddafi continues "to shelter hijackers." Editorial, *The New York Times*, May 14, 1986. It has yet to say anything similar, or anything at all, about those who shelter the hijacker of the

Soviet airliner, or about the long record of hijacking and piracy by the United States' Israeli clients.

78. Abraham Sofaer, *Foreign Affairs*, Summer 1986.

79. Livia Rokach, *Israel's Sacred Terrorism*, a study based on Moshe Sharett's personal diary (AAUG, 1980), p. 20f.; "Sixty Minutes," CBS, 7 p.m., Jan. 19, 1986.

80. Sune Persson, *Mediation and Assassination* (London, 1979); Michael Bar-Zohar, *Ben-Gurion: A Biography* (Delacorte, 1978), pp. 180-81; Stephen Green, *Taking Sides* (Morrow, 1984), p. 38f.; Kimche, *Seven Fallen Pillars* (Secker & Warburg, 1953), pp. 272-73.

81. *The Globe & Mail* (Toronto), Oct. 9, 1985.

82. *The New York Times*, Sept. 27, 1985, a picture caption without a story; *The Asian Wall St. Journal*, Aug. 22, cited by Alexander Cockburn, *The Nation*, Sept. 2, 1985; Housego, *The New York Times Book Review*, July 20, 1986. In France, another terrorist state, there was virtually no protest over the atrocity or the punitive acts taken by France against New Zealand. Says a report from Paris after the settlement with New Zealand: "The action called forth not self-criticism but patriotism. In France's view, New Zealand and its Prime Minister, David Lange, quickly became villains for holding the two agents, unjustly detained, in the common view here, for the crime of having served the national interest. In France, little was made in the press of the death of the Greenpeace crew member, or the fact that the sovereignty of New Zealand had been violated." Despite promises of the socialist government to take "legal action" if "criminal acts" had been committed, "the only legal action taken was against several members of the French government for disclosing information to the press," and "there has been no public investigation" (*The New York Times*, July 30, 1986). A demonstration organised in Paris after the sinking of the ship brought out 150 people and one noted intellectual, René Dumont. Though well attended by the media, the event was given no coverage by TV and the press, including the socialist press and *Libération*. *Le Monde* withheld its four-line announcement of the rally until after it was held. French Greens and peace groups were "hesitant to challenge the mass chauvinism revealed in France by the Greenpeace affair," while the Socialist Party congress gave "a hero's welcome" to Minister Hernu, who was officially responsible for the atrocity (Diana Johnstone and Elizabeth Schilling, *In These Times*, Oct. 23, 1985).
    French terrorism against Greenpeace began with its first

protest over French nuclear testing in its Pacific colonies in 1972, when a French mine-sweeper rammed and nearly sank its yacht, and commandos "swarmed aboard, savagely beat and nearly blinded [Greenpeace director] David McTaggart and one other male crew member with rubber truncheons" (James Ridgeway, *The Village Voice*, Oct. 8, 1985, noting also Soviet harrassment of Greenpeace).

83. See my article, "Watergate: A Skeptical View," *The New York Review*, Sept. 20, 1973; editorial, *More*, Dec. 1975; and introduction to N. Blackstock, ed., *COINTELPRO* (Vintage, 1976).

84. Shultz, *The Boston Globe*, June 25, 1984; *The New York Times*, June 25, 1984, Dec. 30, 1983; AP, *The Boston Globe*, April 23, 1984, *The New York Times*, April 1, 1984; *The International Herald Tribune*, May 5, 1986; Colin Nickerson, *The Boston Globe*, Feb. 3, 1986, on the convention; *Africasia*, July 1985, for details on the captured South African commandos, an episode largely ignored in the United States. On the airliners, see *The Boston Globe, The New York Times, The Washington Post*, Nov. 11, 1983; *The Boston Globe*, Feb. 21, 1984. These barely noted incidents occurred in the midst of the mass hysteria over the shooting down of KAL 007 by the USSR, which merited seven full pages in the densely-printed *Times* index in September 1983 alone.

85. Barry Munslow and Phil O'Keefe, *Third World Quarterly*, Jan. 1984.

86. Dan Fisher, *The Los Angeles Times*, June 21; McGrory, *The Boston Globe*, June 21; David Adams, *The New Statesman*, April 19; *The New York Times*, June 21, 1985. On Ansar, see *The Fateful Triangle*, p. 231f.; interview, *Hotam*, April 11, 1986. See also Amnesty International, "The detention of Palestinians and Lebanese in the military prison of Atlit" (in Israel), April 18, 1984, on the detention of Palestinians and Lebanese transferred from southern Lebanon and held incommunicado without means of communication with families or the Red Cross, denied lawyers and evidence concerning their detention and removal to Israel in violation of international law.

87. *The Los Angeles Times*, July 1, 1985.

88. David Ignatius, *The Wall St. Journal*, June 18, 1985.

89. *The New York Times*, June 21, June 18, July 1, 1985.

90. Bernard Lewis, *The New York Review*, Aug. 15; *The New Republic*, July 8; Reagan, Address to the American Bar Association, July 8 (*The Boston Globe*, July 9); Podhoretz, *The Los Angeles Times*, June 26; *The New York Times*, July 2, 1985.

91. Thomas Friedman, *The New York Times*, June 23; *The New York Times*, June 19, 1985.

92. AP, *The Boston Globe*, July 4; Friedman, *The New York Times*, July 4; *The Boston Globe*, July 4, 1985.

93. John Cooley, *Green March, Black September* (Frank Cass, London, 1973), p. 197; see *The Fateful Triangle, op. cit.*, and Beilin, *op. cit.*, for many similar statements.

94. *The Fateful Triangle, op. cit.*, pp. 181-82.

95. Rabin, speaking to the Knesset, *Hadashot*, March 27, 1985; Tamari, interview, *Monitin*, Oct. 1985. On the perception of soldiers, see the excerpts from the Israeli press translated in *The Fateful Triangle*, which differ from the material offered in *hasbara* exercises in the U.S. (see the preface, note 12). Or the comments by paratrooper Ari Shavit on the 1978 invasion of Lebanon, presented in *Koteret Rashit* (May 13, 1986) as a counterpart to a discussion of the operation by the military command, recalling the "kind of ecstasy" with which heavily armed units poured fire into villages, or anywhere, after it had "become clear that there would be no war here" but rather something more "like a hike." No doubt the truth about other armies is similar, but they do not bask in fables about "purity of arms."

96. Rokach, *op. cit.*; Uri Milshtein, *Al Hamishmar*, Sept. 21, 1983; Kennett Love, *Suez* (McGraw-Hill, 1969), pp. 10f., 61-62.

97. *The New York Times*, Dec. 4, 1984. On the scholarly record, see, for example, my *Towards a New Cold War, op. cit.*, p. 331, discussing Nadav Safran, *Israel: The Embattled Ally* (Harvard, 1978).

98. *The Los Angeles Times*, Nov. 24; *The Boston Globe*, Dec. 19; *The New York Times*, Dec. 20; *The Boston Globe*, Dec. 20, 1983.

99. *The Globe & Mail* (Toronto), July 11; *The Boston Globe*, July 24; *The New York Times*, July 24; *The Boston Herald*, July 25, 1985; *The New York Times*, Jan. 5, 6; *The Boston Globe*, Jan. 5, 6, 1984.

100. James Markham, *The New York Times*, Dec. 3, 1975, giving casualty estimates from Lebanese and Palestinian sources. *The New York Times*, March 23, 1985; *The New York Times*, Dec. 3, 4, 1975.

101. *Time*, March 5, 1973; *The New York Times*, Feb. 22, 1973, giving the number killed as fifteen.

102. There was no supporting evidence in the case of the Libyan jet, but the Soviet allegation may be correct, though it obviously

provides no justification for the atrocity; see R.W. Johnson, *Shoot-Down* (Viking, 1986), a study particularly interesting for its dissection of U.S. government lies. The dismissive American reviews are revealing. Joel Brinkley writes that the book is "flawed" because of its "strident tone" of "disdain bordering on contempt" for major figures in the Reagan Administration, and states falsely that it largely derives from the American press (*The New York Times Book Review*, July 20, 1986). Douglas Feaver claims that Johnson "discredits his thesis with disinformation of his own on points that are easily checked," noting that on page 2 he quotes the International Civil Aviation Organization's report only in part (*Book World, Washington Post Weekly*, July 7, 1986). As is also "easily checked," Johnson quotes the sentence Feaver cites in full on page 234, where it is relevant, quoting on page 2 only the parts that are relevant there.

103. *The New York Times*, Feb. 22, 23; editorial, Feb. 23; Feb. 25, 26, 1973. Amiram Cohen, *Hotam*, Feb. 10, 1984. The incident was briefly recalled during the KAL 007 affair, evoking false claims by apologists for Israeli atrocities that Israel "immediately accepted responsibility" and "paid reparations"; Michael Curtis, letter, *The New York Times*, Oct. 2; Martin Peretz, *The New Republic*, Oct. 24, 1983.

104. See note 85. For comparison of the reaction to the two events, see Robert Scheer, *The Manchester Guardian Weekly*, Sept. 25, 1983; for discussion of other similar incidents, also passed over lightly in the U.S. given the agent of the atrocity, see my "1984: Orwell's and Ours," *Thoreau Quarterly*, Winter/ Spring 1984, and "Notes on Orwell's Problem" in *Knowledge of Language* (Praeger, 1986).

105. On the Lydda-Ramle expulsions, see Benny Morris, *Middle East Journal*, Winter 1986; on the other cases, see my *Fateful Triangle, Turning the Tide*, and sources cited; Schocken, *Foreign Affairs*, Fall 1984. On efforts to assassinate the Palestinian political leadership in 1948, organised by Moshe Dayan, see Uri Milshtein, *Al Hamishmar*, Sept. 21, 1983; *Hadashot*, Jan. 11, 1985. A recently discovered Israeli intelligence report of June 30, 1948, concludes that of the 391,000 Arab refugees (152,000 from outside the area assigned to Israel in the U.N. Partition recommendation), at least seventy percent fled as a result of Jewish military operations (primarily Haganah/IDF), including direct expulsion, an apparent underestimate, Benny Morris observes in his analysis. The report also notes that this

took place in the face of intense efforts of the Arab leadership to stem the flow. He also notes that the "circumstances of the second half of the exodus," from July to October, "are a different story"; "after June '48 there were many more planned expulsions" (*Middle Eastern Studies* (London), Jan. 1986; interview with Haim Bar'am, *Kol Ha'ir*, May 9, 1986).

106. The *Liberty* knew that it had been under surveillance by the Israeli air force, but did not suspect at first that this U.S. ally could be the attacker. The ship sent a request for air support to the Sixth Fleet off Naples, and nuclear-armed jets were dispatched "authorised to use force including destruction if necessary" (in the words of the official Naval Court of Inquiry), but not knowing whom they were to attack. They were recalled under direct order from the Pentagon, narrowly averting a nuclear war. It is testimony to the "special relationship" between Israel and the U.S. that this affair has been effectively covered up for many years; one can hardly imagine any other state attacking an American ship in international waters in this manner with complete impunity. The varying Israeli versions of the event make interesting reading. For a review of several of them (including the only account to have appeared in a major U.S. journal, a shameful cover-up by Ze'ev Schiff and Hirsh Goodman in *The Atlantic Monthly*), see James Ennes, "The USS Liberty: Back in the News," *American-Arab Affairs*, Winter 1985-86. Perhaps the most intriguing is that of Yitzhak Rabin, then Chief of Staff, who describes the attack as "the most alarming development in the entire campaign," during which he experienced "sheer terror." He then proceeds to place it very carefully on June 7 (it was June 8), an inconceivable error, which can only be understood as an effort to obscure the apparent reason for the attack: to conceal from the U.S. the planned invasion of Syria after the ceasefire. Rabin, *Memoirs, op. cit.*, p. 108f.

107. On the southern Lebanon case, see Mark Bruzonsky, *Middle East International*, May 16, 1986; also *The Boston Globe*, April 15; David Shipler, *The New York Times*, April 16, 1986. See *The Houston Chronicle* (AP), May 18, (UPI) May 21, 1984, on the case of New Mexico businessman Mike Mansour, who was jailed for twenty-two days, and, he alleges, tortured and forced to sign a confession, which he repudiates.

108. Robert Tucker, *Commentary*, Oct. 1982.

109. Dario Fernandez-Morera, *History of European Ideas*, Vol. 6, No. 4, 1985.

CHAPTER THREE
Libya in U.S. Demonology

Within the American doctrinal system, no one so epitomises "the evil scourge of terrorism" as Muammar Qaddafi, the "mad dog" of the Arab world, and Libya under his leadership has become the very model of a terrorist state.

The description of Libya under Qaddafi as a terrorist state is certainly just. Amnesty International lists the killings of fourteen Libyan citizens by this terrorist state, four abroad, through 1985, the major acts of terrorism plausibly attributed to Libya.[1] In the course of the hysteria orchestrated to serve other ends, all sorts of charges have been made, but the record confirms the April 1986 statement of a senior U.S. intelligence official that until "a few weeks ago," Qaddafi "had used his people primarily to assassinate Libyan dissidents."[2] "A few weeks ago," this intelligence official continues, Qaddafi "made a clear decision to target Americans."

This alleged decision, which has assumed the aura of indubitable fact within the indoctrination system, though no credible evidence has yet been provided to substantiate it (as we shall see), followed the Gulf of Sidra incident, when a U.S. air and naval armada sank Libyan vessels, killing many, and is entirely legitimate, indeed much belated, under the cynical doctrines professed by the United States executive and endorsed by respected commentators, some already cited, others to which we turn directly.

Amnesty International reports that Libya's terrorist killings began in early 1980, at the time when Jimmy Carter launched the terrorist war in El Salvador with José Napoleon Duarte volunteering to serve as a cover to ensure that arms would flow to the killers.

While Libya was killing fourteen of its own citizens, along with a handful of others, the U.S. client regime of El Salvador killed some fifty thousand of its citizens in the course of what Bishop Rivera y Damas, who succeeded the assassinated Archbishop Romero, described in October 1980, after seven months of terror, as "a war of extermination and genocide against a defenseless civilian population."[3] The security forces who perform these necessary chores were hailed by Duarte, a few weeks later, for their "valiant service alongside the people against subversion" while he conceded that "the masses were with the guerrillas" when this exercise began under the Carter-Duarte alliance. Duarte expressed this praise for the mass murderers as he was sworn in as president of the Junta in an effort to lend it legitimacy and ensure the flow of arms after the murder of four American churchwomen, an act generally regarded in the United States as improper, though justifications were offered even for this atrocity by Jeane Kirkpatrick and Alexander Haig.

Meanwhile, the media assured us that "there is no real argument that most of the estimated 10,000 political fatalities in 1980 were victims of government forces or irregulars associated with them" (The Washington Post), though it was later quietly conceded that at the time, officials of the Carter Administration were informing the media that "security forces were responsible for 90 percent of the atrocities," not "'uncontrollable' right-wing bands" as the press had been reporting.[4]

From the earliest days of the Carter-Reagan terrorist operations in El Salvador, Duarte's primary role has been to ensure that there is no impediment to the slaughter while denying well-documented atrocities or justifying them on the grounds that the victims are "communists." He has played this role to mounting applause in the United States, across the political spectrum, as the savage assault against the civilian population had its intended effect of destroying the threat of meaningful democracy that had emerged in the 1970s with the rise of church-based self-help groups, peasant associations, unions, and other "popular organisations."

The conservative Central America correspondent of the London *Spectator* observes that the death squads "did exactly what they were supposed to do: they decapitated the trade unions and mass organisations" and caused the survivors "either to flee the country or to join the guerrillas," at which point the U.S. war against the rural population moved into high gear, with ample terror and massacre.

It is only natural, then, that the editors of *The New Republic*, who had urged Reagan to pursue the slaughter with no concern for human rights ("there are higher American priorities") and "regardless of how many are murdered," should now look with pleasure at these accomplishments in El Salvador, which is "the real model for supporting the push toward democracy in our sphere." The continuing terror, which is documented by Americas Watch, Amnesty International, and—very rarely—by the media, is a matter of utter indifference in the United States.[5]

The slaughter in El Salvador is not mere state terrorism on a dramatic scale, but international terrorism, given the organisation, supply, training, and direct participation by the Ruler of the Hemisphere. The same is true of the massacre of some seventy thousand Guatemalans in the same years, when U.S. arms to the murderers flowed at close to the normal level contrary to what is commonly alleged. To implement the slaughter more efficiently, though, it was necessary to call in U.S. proxies—the neo-Nazi Argentine generals, Taiwan, and primarily Israel, which lent its expert services enthusiastically to the cause; the U.S. government also constructed an arms pipeline involving Belgium and other collaborators, under the illegal direction of the Pentagon and the CIA, as a supplement. Meanwhile, as the terror reached its peak of savagery, Reagan and his associates extolled the killers and torturers for their human rights improvements and "total dedication to democracy," dismissing the flood of documentation on atrocities as a "bum rap."[6]

115

U.S. international terrorism in El Salvador is hailed as a splendid achievement across the mainstream political spectrum in the United States because it laid the basis for what is called "democracy" in Western parlance: namely, the rule of elite groups serving the needs of the Global Enforcer with the public reduced to occasional ratification of elite decision now that the popular organisations, which might have provided a basis for meaningful democracy, have been "decapitated" and decimated.

In 1982 and 1984 the United States organised what Edward Herman and Frank Brodhead call "demonstration elections" to pacify the home front, carried out in an atmosphere of "terror and despair, macabre rumour and grisly reality," in the words of observers from the British Parliamentary Human Rights Group. The U.S. press, however, lauded this demonstration of American passionate commitment to democracy, as *Pravda* perhaps also does under similar circumstances.[7]

Guatemala is also considered a success, for similar reasons. When half the population is virtually marched to the polls after it has been properly traumatised by U.S.-backed violence, enlightened American commentators are overjoyed at this renewed demonstration of the U.S. love for democracy. They are untroubled by the rise in death-squad killings, the open recognition by the newly-elected president that he can do nothing given the roots of actual power in the military and the oligarchy and that the civilian government are merely "the managers of bankruptcy and misery,"[8] and the fact that the reaction in the United States helps convert the elections into a means for the U.S. to participate more fully in state terror and repression, as in El Salvador. In fact, elections in U.S. terror states are often a mixed blessing or an outright disaster for the domestic population, for this essential reason.

These two examples, of course, represent only a part of the U.S. role in international terrorism during the 1980s, and the grisly record goes back many years.

"The striking feature of Libyan atrocities," two commentators observe in reviewing the Amnesty International study of state terror, "is that they are the only ones whose numbers are sufficiently limited that the individual cases can be enumerated," in striking contrast to Argentina, Indonesia, and the Central American states where the emperor molests the world.[9]

In short, Libya is indeed a terrorist state. But in the world of international terrorism, it is hardly even a bit player.

There remain innocent souls who believe that it is possible to find a level of vulgarity and apologetics for mass slaughter and terror that will not be surpassed in respectable Western publications. They can be disabused of such illusions by consideration of numerous examples during the worst years of the terror in Central America,[10] or by turning to the "neoconservative" journal *The National Interest*, where they can read, in a critique of *The Washington Post* for being soft on Libya, that

> There is no doubt that if, for example, the government of José Napoleon Duarte in El Salvador or any recent government in Turkey had carried out anywhere near the number of executions that Qaddafi has, the *Post* would have provided us with great detail, and would have reported the existence of considerable opposition.[11]

Not only is "terrorism" defined for ideological serviceability, as I discussed earlier, but standards of evidence are also conveniently set so as to achieve the emperor's goals. To demonstrate Libya's role as a state terrorist, the flimsiest evidence, or none at all, will suffice. The headline of a *New York Times* editorial justifying the U.S. terrorist attack that killed some one hundred people in Libya (according to press reports from the scene) reads: "To Save the Next Natasha Simpson." The reference is to the eleven-year-old American girl who was one of the victims of the terrorist attacks in the Rome and Vienna airports on December 27, 1985; these victims entitle us to bomb Libyan cities "to discourage state-supported terrorism," the editors of *The Times* solemnly declare. It is only a minor defect that no evidence has been presented to implicate Libya in these actions.

The Italian and Austrian governments stated that the terrorists were trained in Syrian-controlled areas of Lebanon and had come via Damascus, a conclusion reiterated by the Israeli defense minister, Yitzhak Rabin.

Four months later, in response to U.S. claims about Libyan involvement in the Vienna attack, the Austrian minister of the interior stated that "there is not the slightest evidence to implicate Libya," again citing Syria as the connection and adding that Washington had never presented the evidence of Libyan complicity it had promised to provide to the Austrian authorities. He also added the correct but—in the U.S.—inexpressible comment that the problem of Lebanese-based terrorism lies largely in the failure to solve the Palestine problem, which has led desperate people to turn to violence, exactly the result intended by U.S.-Israeli terrorism, as discussed in Chapter Two.[12]

A few months later, Italy's minister of the interior, while signing an agreement with the U.S. for cooperation in "the fight against terrorism," reiterated the position expressed by Italy "since January" that they suspected a Syrian source for the Rome and Vienna attacks. The Times reported his statement, but without feeling any need to comment on the righteous blow of retaliation against Libya that they had applauded in April, which is sheer unprovoked terrorism according to their news report.[13]

If an individual implicated in a terrorist act once paid a visit to Libya, or is alleged to have received training or funds from Libya in the past, that suffices for condemnation of Qaddafi as a "mad dog" who must be eradicated. The same standards would implicate the CIA in the murderous exploits of Cuban exiles, among numerous others.

Keeping just to 1985, one of the suspects in the bombing of the Air India jumbo jet near Ireland that was the year's worst terrorist act, killing 329 people, was trained at an anti-communist school for mercenaries in Alabama. U.S. Attorney-General Meese, visiting India nine months later, made a barely-reported statement that the U.S. was taking steps "to prevent terrorists from obtaining training or resources in the United States," referring to the private military training camps that India has charged have trained Sikh extremists. Meese's statement is untrue, as far as is known, though the press has not been interested in investigating.[14]

118

The terrorist action that took the most lives in the Middle East in 1985 was a car-bombing in Beirut in March that killed eighty people and wounded two hundred. It was carried out by a Lebanese intelligence unit trained and supported by the CIA, in an effort to kill a Shi'ite leader who was believed to have been involved in "terrorist attacks against U.S. installations" in Beirut.[15] The term "terrorism" is commonly used by foreign armies in reference to actions against them by the local population, who see them as an occupying force imposing a detested political settlement instituted by a foreign invasion, in this case Israel's "New Order."

By the standards of evidence used in the case of Libya, the U.S. was once again the world's leading terrorist power in 1985, even if we exclude the wholesale terrorism ruled ineligible by the propaganda system.

Continuing to 1986, the most serious terrorist acts in the Mediterranean region as of the time of writing—apart from Israel's continuing terrorism in Lebanon—are the U.S. bombing of Libya and the bombings in Syria which, according to the radio station of Lebanon President Amin Gemayel's Phalangist Party, killed more than 150 people in April. These bombings were blamed by Syria on Israeli agents, with no reported evidence but no less credibility than similar U.S. charges against whoever happens to be the villain of the day—and, incidentally, not falling within "the evil scourge of terrorism."[16]

The U.S., of course, disclaims responsibility for the actions of terrorists it has trained: Cubans, Lebanese, mass murderers such as Rios Montt in Guatemala, and numerous others in Latin America and elsewhere.

In the case of the Lebanon bombing, for example, the CIA denied involvement, though this denial was "disputed by some Administration and Congressional officials who said that the agency was working with the group at the time of the bombing." This conclusion was also drawn by a *Washington Post* inquiry, which determined that Washington cancelled the covert operation after the bombing, conducted without CIA authorisation.[17]

Even if we accept the claim that the CIA did not authorise the bombing and was no longer involved with the terrorist group it had trained, the government's excuse is readily dismissed by the standards applied to official enemies by apologists for U.S. and Israeli terrorism, both in the government and in the media. Recall that "the larger moral responsibility for atrocities... is *all* Yasir Arafat's" because "he was, and remains, the founding father of contemporary Palestinian violence," and thus the U.S. will hold Arafat "accountable for acts of international terrorism" quite generally, whether he is involved or not.[18] Hence "the larger moral responsibility" in the cases mentioned and much else is "*all* Washington's," whatever the facts about direct involvement.

As noted in the preface, the Reagan campaign against "international terrorism" was a natural choice for the propaganda system in furtherance of its basic agenda: expansion of the state sector of the economy; transfer of resources from the poor to the rich; and a more "activist" (i.e., terrorist and aggressive) foreign policy.

Such policies require that the public be frightened into obedience by some terrible enemy threatening to destroy us, but it is necessary to avoid, as too dangerous, direct confrontation with the Great Satan himself. International terrorism by the Evil Empire's proxies is the obvious candidate, and the Administration's public relations specialists turned at once to the task of concocting the appropriate web of half-truths and outright deceit, correctly anticipating that the charade would be taken seriously by sober commentators.

Libya fit the need perfectly. Qaddafi is easy to hate, particularly against the background of rampant anti-Arab racism in the United States and the deep commitment of the educated classes, with only the rarest of exceptions, to U.S.-Israeli rejectionism and violence. He has created an ugly and repressive society, and is indeed guilty of retail terrorism, primarily against Libyans, as noted.

Qaddafi's execution of Libyan dissidents, his major recorded terrorist acts, might have been prevented, according to U.S. and Israeli intelligence analysts, but with the possible consequence of revealing that the (apparently quite transparent)

Libyan codes had been broken. "An Israeli analyst put it more bluntly: 'Why expose our sources and methods for the sake of some Libyans?'."[19] Libya is weak and defenseless so that martial law flourishes and, when needed, murder of Libyans can be conducted with impunity.

The glorious military victory in Grenada, a culmination of the extreme hostility and aggressiveness of the Carter and Reagan Administrations after the Bishop government threatened to consider the needs of the poor majority, served similar ends.

The point is readily perceived abroad. American journalist Donald Neff, writing in a British publication about the March 1986 Gulf of Sidra incident, comments that

> this was less of a Rambo-style operation than a demonstration of the bully on the block picking a fight. It was typical of Reagan. In his five years in office, he has repeatedly got away with lording it over little guys. He did this time too.

It is an interesting fact about American culture that this regular show of cowardice and two-bit thuggery seems to strike a responsive chord, as it sometimes does abroad as well. For example, Paul Johnson denounces the "distasteful whiff of pure cowardice in the air" as "the wimps" raise doubts about the U.S. bombing of "terrorist bases" (that is, civilian targets) in Libya. Johnson admires "the strength of the Cowboy," who demonstrates his courage by sending his bombers to murder defenseless civilians.[20]

The public relations specialists of the Reagan Administration understood the utility of the Libyan enemy and wasted little time in confronting this dangerous foe. Libya was at once designated as a prime agent of the Soviet-inspired "terror network," and in July 1981 a CIA plan to overthrow and possibly kill Qaddafi with a paramilitary campaign of terror within Libya was leaked to the press.[21]

We may note parenthetically that by U.S. standards this plan authorised Qaddafi to carry out acts of terror against American targets in "self-defense against future attack"— the words of White House spokesman Larry Speakes presenting

121

the official justification for the bombing of Tripoli and Benghazi. The same justification was reiterated at the United Nations by Vernon Walters and Herbert Okun. The Administration even had the gall to argue that this right—which not even Hitler claimed and which, if proclaimed by other violent states, would tear to shreds what little remains of global order and international law—is in accord with the United Nations Charter. No form of legal sophistry can bridge that gap, but the Administration rightly assumed that "it would play well in Peoria"—and in Cambridge, New York, and Washington. Reagan was duly acclaimed by Anthony Lewis for his reliance "on a legal argument that violence against the perpetrators of repeated violence is justified as an act of self-defense." Why the U.S. justified the attack "on the basis of pre-empting an attack, which could be seen as a form of self-defense, [rather] than as a retaliatory action" was explained by a State Department official. The U.N. Charter, the official noted, expressly forbids the use of force except in self-defense—in fact, self-defense against armed attack, until the U.N. acts after a formal request to the Security Council by the country that regards itself as the victim of a sudden and overwhelming armed attack.

While the "legal argument" was admired at home, it was generally dismissed abroad, where few could be found who would disagree with Canada's former U.N. ambassador, George Ignatieff, a member of the first Canadian delegation to the U.N. and now Chancellor of the University of Toronto. Ignatieff rejected the appeal to the right of self-defense established in the U.N. Charter as without merit.[22]

In August 1981, the anti-Qaddafi message "was reinforced by the trap laid for Libya in the Gulf of Sidra," a trap "elaborately planned on the U.S. side" with the intent of a confrontation in which Libyan jets could be shot down—as they were, Edward Haley observes in his bitterly anti-Qaddafi study of U.S. relations with Libya. One specific purpose, Haley plausibly argues, was to

exploit the "Libyan menace" in order to win support for steps [the Administration] wished to take in pursuit of Secretary Haig's "strategic consensus" against the Soviet

Union, and as an element in the arrangements necessary for the creation of a Rapid Deployment Force [an intervention force targeted primarily at the Middle East].

In November, the Administration concocted a ludicrous tale about Libyan hit-men roaming the streets of Washington to assassinate Reagan, eliciting feverish media commentary along with some scepticism, which was quite limited at the time.

When questioned about the plot, Reagan stated: "We have the evidence, and [Qaddafi] knows it."[23]

The story faded away when its purpose had been served, and the press was sufficiently disciplined so as not to report the exposure in the British press that the "assassins" on the official U.S. list, which was leaked in England, were prominent members of the (passionately anti-Libyan) Lebanese Amal, including its leader, Nabih Berri, and the elderly religious leader of the Shi'ite community.[24]

Other tales included a Libyan threat to invade the Sudan across six hundred miles of desert (with the Egyptian and U.S. air forces helpless to impede this outrage), and a plot to overthrow the government of the Sudan in February 1983, conveniently discovered at a moment when the Administration's reactionary constituency was charging it with insufficient militancy. The plot was so subtle that Sudanese and Egyptian intelligence knew nothing about it, as U.S. reporters who took the trouble to go to Khartoum to investigate quickly discovered.

The U.S. responded to the fabricated plot with an elaborate show of force, enabling Secretary of State Shultz, who had been denounced as too faint-hearted, to strike heroic poses on television while announcing that Qaddafi "is back in his box where he belongs" because Reagan acted "quickly and decisively" against this threat to world order. Again, the episode was forgotten once its purposes had been served. There has been a series of similar examples. The media have generally played their appointed role, with only occasional demurrers.[25]

The events of March-April 1986 fit the familiar pattern to perfection. The Gulf of Sidra operation in March was plainly timed to stir up jingoist hysteria just prior to the crucial Senate vote on *contra* aid, coinciding with a fabricated Nicaraguan "invasion" of Honduras, an inspired public relations operation that succeeded brilliantly as demonstrated by the enraged reaction of Congressional doves and the media fairly generally (see Chapter Two). The charade also permitted the Administration to provide $20 million in military aid to Honduras, which Honduras officially maintains it did not request, and which has no doubt been conveniently "lost" in the *contra* camps—yet another method by which the lawless band in Washington evades the weak Congressional restrictions on their thuggery.[26] The Gulf of Sidra provocation, too, was a success, enabling U.S. forces to sink several Libyan boats, killing more than fifty Libyans, and, it was hoped, to incite Qaddafi to acts of terror against Americans, as was subsequently claimed.

While the U.S. forces were successful in killing many Libyans, they were singularly unable to rescue survivors. The task was apparently not impossible, however, since sixteen survivors of the U.S. attack were rescued from a lifeboat by a Spanish oil tanker.[27]

The official purpose of the U.S. military operation was to establish the right of passage in the Gulf of Sidra—which is perfect nonsense, since dispatch of a naval flotilla was hardly the necessary or appropriate means to achieve this end: a declaration would have sufficed. Were further steps deemed necessary for some reason, lawful means were readily available. If someone has a dispute with his neighbour over property rights, there are two ways to proceed: one is to take the matter to the courts; the second is to pick up a gun and kill the neighbour. The first option was surely available in the case of the Gulf of Sidra.

Since there is plainly no urgency, it was possible to resort to legal means to establish the right of innocent passage. But a lawless and violent terrorist state will naturally observe different priorities. Asked why the U.S. did not take the issue to the World Court, Brian Hoyle, director of the Office of Ocean Law and Policy at the State Department, said that the case "would have taken years and years. I don't think we could live with this"[28]—given the evident necessity for

U.S. naval armadas to operate in the Gulf of Sidra if the United States is to survive as a nation.

The U.S. position is dubious on narrower grounds. The press continually speaks of "the law of the sea," but the United States is hardly on firm grounds in appealing to this doctrine if only because the Reagan Administration rejected the Law of the Sea Treaty. Furthermore, Libya shot at U.S. planes, not U.S. ships, and "the law of the air" is far from well established. States make various claims in this regard. The U.S., for example, claims a two-hundred-mile Air Defense Identification Zone within which it has the right to exercise "self-defense" against intruding aircraft judged to be hostile. There is no doubt that U.S. aircraft were well within two hundred miles of Libyan territory— forty miles, the Pentagon claims—and that they were hostile, so that by U.S. standards, Libya was within its rights to intercept them. The point was noted by the conservative legal scholar Alfred Rubin of the Fletcher School at Tufts University, who commented that "by sending in aircraft we went beyond what we were clearly authorized to do under the Law of the Sea" in "an unnecessary provocation."[29] But for a gangster state, such matters are irrelevant, and the exercise was a success— domestically, at least.

The extent of the provocation in the Gulf of Sidra was made clear by Pentagon spokesman Robert Sims, who "said that U.S. policy is to shoot at any Libyan boat that enters international waters in the Gulf of Sidra for as long as the U.S. naval exercise in that region continues—no matter how far away the boat might be from U.S. ships." "Given the 'hostile intent' displayed by Libya when it tried to shoot down U.S. warplanes," Sims states, any Libyan military vessel is "a threat to our forces."[30] In short, the U.S. maintains the right to fire in "self-defense" at any Libyan vessel that approaches its naval armada off the Libyan coast, but Libya does not have a right of self-defense in air space comparable to that claimed by the U.S.

There is more to the story. British correspondent David Blundy interviewed British engineers in Tripoli who were repairing the Russian-installed radar system there. One, who says he was monitoring the incident throughout on the radar screens (which, contrary to Pentagon claims, were not rendered inoperative), reports that

> he saw American warplanes cross not only into the 12 miles of Libyan territorial waters, but over Libyan land as well.... "I watched the planes fly approximately eight miles into Libyan air space," he said. "I don't think the Libyans had any choice but to hit back. In my opinion they were reluctant to do so."

The engineer added that

> American warplanes made their approach using a normal civil airline traffic route and followed in the wake of a Libyan airliner, so that its radar blip would mask them on the Libyan radar screen.[31]

No hint of this information appeared in the U.S. media, to my knowledge, apart from a typically excellent report by Alexander Cockburn, playing his usual role of personal antidote to media subservience and distortion. Blundy's article was not mysteriously missed by the U.S. press. It was cited by Joseph Lelyveld of *The Times*, but with its crucial contents pointedly ignored.[32]

One likely—and no doubt eagerly awaited—consequence of the Gulf of Sidra operation was to elicit acts of Libyan terrorism in retaliation. These would then have the effect of inducing a state of terror in the United States and, with some luck, in Europe as well, setting the stage for the next escalation.

The bombing of the La Belle discothèque in West Berlin on April 5, with one black American soldier and one Turk killed,[33] was immediately blamed on Libya, and was then used as the pretext for the April 14 bombing of Tripoli and Benghazi, with many Libyans killed, apparently mostly civilians (about one hundred, according to the Western press; sixty according to the official Libyan report).

The bombing was neatly timed to take place the day before the expected House vote on *contra* aid. In case the audience missed the point, Reagan's speech writers made it explicit.

Addressing the American Business Conference on April 15, he said:

> And I would remind the House voting this week that this archterrorist has sent $400 million and an arsenal of weapons and advisers into Nicaragua to bring his war home to the United States. He has bragged that he is helping the Nicaraguans because they fight America on its own ground.[34]

The idea that the "mad dog" is bringing his war home to the U.S. by providing arms to people whom the U.S. is attacking with its terrorist proxy army was a nice touch, which passed without notable comment. The public relations operation, however, did not—for once—succeed in steamrollering Congress, though the bombing of Libya did enflame chauvinist passions.

This consequence was perhaps largely attributable to the prevailing anti-Arab racism and the relative absence of any sane reaction to earlier episodes of manufactured hysteria over Qaddafi's real and alleged crimes.

The April 14 attack was the first bombing in history staged for prime-time teleivson. As the subsequently published record shows, the bombing raids were carefully timed to begin precisely at 7 p.m. Eastern Standard Time—as they did[35]; that is, precisely at the moment when all three national television channels broadcast their major news programmes—which were, of course, pre-empted as agitated anchormen switched to Tripoli for direct eyewitness reports of the exciting events. As soon as the raids ended, the White House had Larry Speakes address a press conference, followed by other dignitaries, ensuring total domination of the propaganda system during the crucial early hours.

One might argue that the Administration took a gamble in this transparent public relations operation, since journalists could have asked some difficult questions. But the White House was justly confident that nothing untoward would occur and its faith in the servility of the media proved to be entirely warranted.

Questions could have been raised, surely. To mention only the most obvious one, Speakes stated that the U.S. knew on April 4 that the East Berlin Libyan "People's Bureau" had informed Tripoli that an attack would take place in Berlin the following day, and that it then informed Tripoli that the La Belle discothèque bombing had taken place, as planned. Thus the U.S. knew on April 4-5 — with certainty, the White House alleged — that Libya was directly responsible for the disco bombing. One might have asked, then, why the reports of U.S. and West German investigations from April 5 to the moment of the attack consistently stated that there were at most suspicions of Libyan involvement. In fact, every journalist listening to the Administration story had in his or her hands — unless we assume the most astonishing imcompetence on the part of the newsrooms — an AP report from Berlin which came across the wires at 6:28 p.m. EST, a half-hour before the bombing, stating that "the Allied military command [in West Berlin] reported no developments in the investigation of the disco bombing" and that "U.S. and West German officials have said Libya—*possibly* through its embassy in Communist-ruled East Berlin—is *suspected* of involvement in the bombing of the La Belle night-club" (my emphasis).[36]

Some journalist might have asked, then, how it is that a few minutes prior to the attack, the U.S. and West Germany still had, at most, *suspicions* of Libyan involvement—as throughout the preceding period—while on April 4-5, ten days earlier, they had certain knowledge of it. But no embarrassing questions were asked then, nor have they been since, and the relevant facts have been largely suppressed.

Reagan stated on the evening of April 14 that "our evidence is direct, it is precise, it is irrefutable"—just as "we have the evidence, and [Qaddafi] knows it" in the case of the Libyan hit-men, not to speak of the Sandinista involvement in drug-peddling, their announcement of a "revolution without frontiers," the support of Helmut Kohl and Bettino Craxi for the Libyan attack (angrily denied by "shocked" officials in Germany and Italy),[37] and numerous other fabrications of an Administration that has surpassed the usual standards of deceit, yet continues "to commit any crime, to lie, to cheat"—in the words of the titular leadership, referring to his Stalinist models—to achieve its ends. It is confident that the occasional exposure in the small print, well after the fact, will not prevent the constant stream of lies from setting the terms of debate and leaving the appropriate impressions firmly implanted.

Beyond the borders, however, discipline did not reign. In Germany, a week after Washington had stated its certain knowledge ten days earlier (April 4-5) of Libyan responsibility for the disco bombing, *Der Spiegel* (April 21) reports that the famed telephone intercepts apparently do not exist and that West Berlin intelligence has only suspicions about Libyan involvement, also suspecting "rival groups of drug dealers" among other possibilities (including Klan or neo-Nazi groups, some suspect; the disco was frequented by black GIs and Third World immigrants). Washington's war is "a means of politics," *Der Spiegel* continues, "insofar as the enemy is as small as Grenada and Libya—and the adversary is as ideal a scoundrel as Qaddafi," and no European leader should have any illusions that Europe's concerns or interests will be considered if the U.S. decides to escalate international violence, even to the level of a final world war, editor Rudolf Augstein adds.[38]

In an interview on April 28 with a reporter for the U.S. Army journal *Stars and Stripes*, Manfred Ganschow, chief of the Berlin Staatschutz and head of the hundred-man team investigating the disco bombing, stated that "I have no more evidence that Libya was connected to the bombing than I had when you first called me two days after the act. Which is none." He agreed that it was "a highly political case" and hinted at considerable scepticism about what "the politicians" were saying and would say about it.[39]

The U.S. press has concealed the doubts expressed by the media and the investigating team in Germany, but the discerning reader will be able to detect them in the reports of the continuing investigation, as suspects alleged to have Syrian and other connections are investigated. The U.S. government claims of "certain knowledge" on April 4-5 have been downgraded with qualifications such as "reportedly" and "alleged," an indication that the media know very well that the claims are dubious or fabricated, but are much too loyal, or too afraid, to say so—and thus, incidentally, to reveal their own complicity in the terrorist bombing.[40] The hesitancy, the qualifications, the backing off from the former confident assertion, and the indirect citation of evidence that undermines Administration claims—these are the devices used by the media to signal that they are well aware that there was never any merit to the case they enthusiastically endorsed when called upon to rally round the flag.

In *The New York Review of Books*, Shaul Bakhash asserts that the Jordanian Hindawi brothers were "responsible for the bombing of the nightclub in West Berlin" and that "there is now persuasive evidence" that they "were recruited by Syria (not by Libya as one might have thought from some official statements at the time)."[41]

Apart from the fact that Bakhash goes well beyond available evidence, this is a curious formulation. It was not a matter of "some official statements" from which "one might have thought" that Libya was involved: rather, *all* official statements, presented with certainty and no qualifications and repeated in this manner by the media until the case began to unravel weeks later, confidently asserted Libyan responsibility and justified the bombing and killing of Libyan civilians on this basis. Furthermore, neither the media backtracking nor this statement draw the obvious conclusion: if the Reagan Administration was lying about its "direct," "precise," and "irrefutable" evidence, then the bombing was simply unprovoked state terrorism—covered up by the loyal media, which avoided the obvious questions at the time of their enthusiastic endorsement of the attack while offering absurd pretexts (e.g., the *Times* editors' fable about "the next Natasha Simpson") in justifying their complicity in terrorism.

The public relations operation was surely a success, at least in the short term, at home. It "is playing well in Peoria," as the press reported, a successful example of "the engineering of democratic consent" that should, as intended, "strengthen President Reagan's hand in dealing with Congress on issues like the military budget and aid to Nicaraguan 'contras'."[42]

For much of the world, the U.S. has become an object of considerable fear, as its "bizarre cowboy leader" engages in acts of "madness" in organising a "band of cutthroats" to attack Nicaragua and playing mad bomber elsewhere, in the words of Canada's leading journal, which is generally restrained and quite pro-U.S.[43]

The Reagan Administration is successfully playing on these fears, exploiting Nixon's "madman" strategy. At the Tokyo Summit of the advanced industrial democracies in May 1986, the Reagan Administration circulated a position paper in which it stated that one reason Europe would be wise to line up in the U.S. crusade is "the need to do something so that the crazy Americans won't take matters into their own hands again." The threat succeeded in eliciting a statement against terrorism mentioning only Libya by name.[44] This explicit threat is invariably ignored as the media exult in the "success" of the Libya bombing in bringing European "wimps" finally to take the measures required to counter the Libyan threat to Western civilisation.

The reaction to the bombing of Libya at home and abroad was sharply different. The twelve-member European Economic Community called upon the U.S. to avoid "further escalation of military tension in the region with all the inherent dangers." A few hours later, U.S. warplanes struck, as West German Foreign Minister Hans-Dietrich Genscher was on his way to Washington to explain the EEC position. His spokesman stated, "We want to do everything we can to avoid a military escalation." The bombing aroused extensive protest throughout most of Europe, including large demonstrations, and evoked editorial condemnation in most of the world. Spain's major newspaper, the independent *El Pais*, condemned the raid:

> The military action of the United States is not only an offence against international law and a grave threat to peace in the Mediterranean, but a mockery of its European allies, who did not find motives for economic sanctions against Libya in a meeting Monday, despite being previously and unsuccessfully pressured to adopt sanctions.

The conservative *South China Morning Post* in Hong Kong wrote that "President Reagan's cure for the 'mad dog of the

Middle East' may prove more lethal than the disease," and his action "may also have lit the fuse to a wider conflagration" in the Middle East. In Mexico City, *El Universal* wrote that the U.S. "has no right to set itself up as the defender of world freedom," urging recourse to legal means through the United Nations. There were many similar reactions.

The U.S. press, in contrast, was overwhelmingly favourable. *The New York Times* wrote that "even the most scrupulous citizen can only approve and applaud the American attacks on Libya," describing this as a just sentence: "...the United States has prosecuted [Qaddafi] carefully, proportionately—and justly." The evidence for Libyan responsibility for the disco bombing has been "now laid out clearly to the public"; "Then came the jury, the European governments to which the United States went out of its way to send emissaries to share evidence and urge concerted action against the Libyan leader."

It is irrelevant, apparently, that the jury was hardly convinced by the evidence, and issued a "judgement" calling on the executioner to refrain from any action—just as it is unnecessary to comment editorially on the fact, now tacitly recognised, that the evidence was of little merit, if any.

Most governments also condemned the action, though not all.

Britain and Canada went along, though the public response was sharply different, and there was support from France in its current mood of Reaganite fanaticism. The government-controlled South African Broadcasting Corporation said the attack "underlines the commitment the leader of the Western world has made to taking positive action against terrorism"; the U.S. was justified in attacking Qaddafi, "whose name is virtually synonymous with international terrorism." In Israel, Prime Minister Shimon Peres stated that the U.S. action was clearly justified in "self-defense":

> If the Libyan Government issues orders to murder American soldiers in Beirut in cold blood, in the middle of the night, what do you expect the United States to do? Sing Hallelujah? Or take action in her defense?

The idea that the U.S. was acting in "self-defense" against an attack on her forces in Beirut two and a half years earlier is an intriguing innovation, even putting aside the circumstances of that earlier act of "terrorism."[45]

In the U.S., Senator Mark Hatfield, one of the few political figures in the country who merits the honourable term "conservative," denounced the U.S. bombing raid "on a nearly deserted Senate floor" and in a letter to *The Times*. Leaders of several major Christian denominations also condemned the bombing.

Jewish leaders generally praised the bombing, however, among them Rabbi Alexander Schindler, president of the Union of American Hebrew Congregations, who "said the U.S. government 'properly and vigorously responded' to the 'mindless terrorism'"of Qaddafi. Harvard international affairs professor Joseph Nye said Reagan had to respond "to the smoking gun of that Berlin thing. What else do you do about state-supported terrorism?"—such as U.S.-supported terrorism in Central America and southern Lebanon, for example, where the "smoking gun" is considerably more in evidence.

Eugene Rostow supported the bombing as "inevitable and overdue," part of a "more active defense against the process of Soviet expansion"—a typical expression of the weird amalgam of mindless jingoism and Maoist fantasy that has attained respectability in current commentary on international affairs.

The "forcible removal of the Qaddafi regime," Rostow explained, "would be fully justified under the existing rules of international law," since Qaddafi "has flagrantly and continually violated these rules." "That being the case, every state injured by Libya's actions has the right, alone or with others, to use whatever force is reasonably necessary to put an end to Libya's illegal behavior. Libya is in the legal position of the Barbary pirates."[46] He urged NATO to "issue a declaration on the responsibility of states for illegal acts committed from their territory."[47] *A fortiori*, then, NATO should condemn the emperor, not just the pirate, and states from Indochina to Central America to the Middle East, among others, should organise to use whatever force is necessary to attack the United States, Israel, and other terrorist states.

For ABC correspondent Charles Glass, who reported the bombing and its aftermath from the scene, the event was symbolised by the handwritten letter of a seven-year-old girl, dug out of the rubble of her home, whose American-educated family he visited. The letter reads:

> Dear Mr. Reagan
> Why did you killl my only sister Rafa and my friend Racha, she is only nine, and my baby doll Strawberry. Is it true you want to kill us all because my father is Palestinian and you want to kill Kadafi because he wants to help us go back to my father's home and land.
> My name is Kinda

Others saw the matter differently. Michael Walzer took issue with Europeans who criticised the bombing of Libya as a case of "state terrorism." This it was not, he declared, "for it was aimed at specific military targets, and the pilots took some risks in their effort to hit those targets and nothing else." If night bombing of a city happens to strike densely-populated residential sections of Tripoli, killing many civilians, that is just the way the cookie crumbles.[49] Perhaps this is what we should expect of the highly-regarded moralist and theorist of just war who assured us that the Israeli invasion of Lebanon can be defended under this concept, that Israel's military operations in southern Lebanon were "a good example of proportionate warfare," and that if civilians are "at risk" during the Israeli bombing of Beirut, then "the responsibility for the risks lies with the PLO."[50]

Media complicity in this act of state terrorism did not end with the patriotic behaviour just reviewed at the time of the bombing, a natural sequel to earlier endorsement of whatever fanciful tales the Administration chose to concoct. It was also necessary to show that the bombing was a success in curbing Libyan terrorism, as proven by the absence of terrorist actions attributed to Qaddafi after the bombing. Of course, to establish the thesis, it is necessary to suppress the fact that neither were there any credible attributions *prior* to the bombing apart from those mentioned earlier, which are clearly irrelevant. The media have again proven themselves quite adequate to the task at hand.

The editors of *The Washington Post* extol the Libya bombing on the grounds that "no new acts of terrorism have been attributed to" Qaddafi, who has now been reduced to a "subdued policy." Still more important is the effect on Western allies, most of whom "needed the shock" delivered by "the example of decisiveness, the undeniable precision of the intelligence, the subsequent demonstration of Libya's isolation and, not least, the fall in tourism"—and, not least, the threat that the "crazy Americans" might flail away with abandon somewhere else (see above), a threat underscored by the dispatch of U.S. naval vessels to within a few miles of the Soviet coastline in the Black Sea at the same time[51]; note that at this late date, the editors still find it possible to refer to "the undeniable precision of the intelligence."

David Ignatius writes that the bombing "worked surprisingly well against Libya's Moammar Gadhafi," accomplishing "some startling—and very beneficial—changes in Libya, the Mideast and Europe." It proved that Qaddafi was "weak, isolated and vulnerable," "so vulnerable, in fact, that American warplanes were able to operate freely within his own, heavily defended airspace"—a glorious victory indeed, and a most surprising discovery about this superpower. To demonstrate "the psychology that had allowed Gadhafi to intimidate much of the world," Ignatius cites no acts—for he knows that there are no credible examples—but instead states, rather lamely, that even if "Libyans may engage in terrorism again, it won't be on the scale they seemed to be embarking on early this year" when "U.S. intelligence learned that Libya had ordered its 'Peoples Bureaus' to mount terrorist attacks in about a dozen cities." A highly competent journalist, Ignatius knows that U.S. government claims about what intelligence had "learned" are worthless; his demonstration of the "success" of the operation in terms of alleged plans aborted is his circumspect way of saying that the consequences of the "ugly act" were nil.[52]

Similarly, George Moffett notes that Libyan terrorist attacks "have all but ceased"—that is, they have been reduced from near zero to near zero—one of the "positive developments" that "appear to vindicate the Reagan administration's policy of military retaliation." His colleague John Hughes observes triumphantly that "since the punitive air strikes against Libya... there have been no major terrorist attacks on Americans directed by Col. Muammar Qaddafi"—just as there were none before, so far as is known.[53]

The message to the state terrorists is clear: We will follow your dictates when you concoct a record of terrorism that has intimidated the world, when you carry out a major terrorist act to punish this outrage, and when you announce that as a result of your heroism, the criminal is subdued. Mere facts will never deter us from our obedience.

For the record, "there have been some 18 anti-American terrorist incidents in Western Europe and the Middle East in the three months since the Libyan raid, compared with about 15 during the 3 ½ months before it," while "in the world as a whole, the rate of anti-American terrorism looks like being little different from last year," *The Economist* observes (while lauding Reagan's act of courage); and the Rand Corporation's leading specialist on terrorism notes that terrorist attacks after the raid persisted at about the same level as before.[54]

Completing the record, on July 3 the FBI released a forty-one-page report reviewing terrorist incidents within the United States in 1985. Seven were listed, with two people killed. In 1984, there were thirteen terrorist acts. The number has dropped each year since 1982, when fifty-one terrorist incidents were recorded.[55]

The media coverage of the FBI report is interesting. The Toronto *Globe & Mail* ran an AP story on July 4 under the headline: "Jewish extremists blamed in 2 deaths." The lead paragraph reads: "Jewish extremists committed four of the seven terrorist acts that killed two people in the United States in 1985, the Federal Bureau of Investigation reported yesterday." The report goes on to provide details of the "incidents attributed to Jewish extremists" which "killed two people and injured nine, the report said" (the two being the only fatalities), along with the other incidents.

The New York Times, in contrast, ran no story on the FBI report. Its only reference to the report is in the eleventh paragraph of a column on July 17, reading: "According to the F.B.I.'s annual report on terrorism, four of seven instances of domestic terrorism in 1985 were believed to involve 'Jewish terrorist groups.' No indictments have resulted from any [of] the investigations." The second national newspaper, *The Washington Post*, ran a story on the FBI report on July 5 headlined "Domestic Terrorism Declined Last Year, FBI Report Shows." It is noted within that "both killings and nine of the injuries were attributed to four terrorist acts by Jewish extremists" (of the seven reported); this is repeated in a July 17 story on the FBI investigation of the murder of Alex Odeh, noting that "Jewish extremist groups are suspects."[56]

These three sentences constitute U.S. national press coverage of the conclusions of the FBI report on sources of domestic terrorism in 1985. I noticed no editorials or other comments calling upon the United States to bomb Tel Aviv or Jerusalem to excise the "cancer" and "subdue" the "mad dogs" who have brought "the evil scourge of terrorism" to its own shores. One may ask why not.

Naturally, Israel disclaims responsibility for the actions of "Jewish extremists" and condemns the terrorist actions, as does Knesset Member Rabbi Kahane whose former associates of the Jewish Defense League are suspected by the FBI of carrying out the actions, just as the U.S. disclaims responsibility for the terrorist acts of those it has trained and encouraged. But as I have already mentioned, these excuses amount to naught by the standards applied to Muammar Qaddafi and Yasser Arafat, who also condemn terrorist actions and deny responsibility for them. Recall again the doctrine that "the larger moral responsibility for atrocities... is *all* Yasir Arafat's" because "he was, and remains, the founding father of contemporary Palestinian violence," and thus the U.S. will hold Arafat "accountable for acts of international terrorism" quite generally, whether he is involved or not.[57]

Hence, "the larger moral responsibility" for the acts of Zionist extremists is *all* Israel's.

The press has regularly dismissed Arafat's condemnation of Palestinian terrorist actions. To mention one particularly striking case, on June 3, 1982, the terrorist group headed by Abu Nidal, who had been condemned to death years earlier by the PLO, attempted to assassinate Israeli Ambassador Shlomo Argov in London, the event that precipitated Israel's invasion of Lebanon—a "retaliation" considered legitimate by the U.S. government, the media, and educated opinion generally. *The Washington Post* commented that the Argov assassination attempt was an "embarrassment" for the PLO, which "claims to represent all Palestinians, but... tends to be selective about accepting responsibility for acts of Palestinian violence" (June 7, 1982).

If a terrorist act by a Palestinian group at war with the PLO is an "embarrassment" for the PLO on these grounds, then plainly terrorist acts by Zionist extremists in the U.S., killing two and wounding nine, are an "embarrassment" for Israel, which is, by law, "the State of the Jewish people," including those in the diaspora (not the state of its citizens, one-sixth of whom are non-Jews). Hence by the logic of the U.S. government, noted commentators, and the media quite generally, the U.S. is certainly entitled, if not obligated, to bomb Tel Aviv "in self-defense against future attacks."

One might suspect that it was "embarrassment" over this logical consequence of their proclaimed doctrines that explains the curious treatment of the FBI report in the U.S. media, though this surmise probably underestimates the capacity to deal with self-contradiction. One may also imagine the media reaction had the majority of terrorist actions in the U.S., including all fatalities, been committed by Arab-Americans associated with extremist elements of the PLO or suspected of being part of a terrorist group founded by a member of the Libyan government.

The U.S. bombing of Libya had nothing to do with "terrorism," even in the cynical Western sense of the word. In fact, it was clear enough that the Gulf of Sidra operation and the bombing of Libyan cities would if anything incite such retail terrorism, one major reason that the likely targets in Europe pleaded with the U.S. to refrain from such action.

This is hardly the first time that violent actions have been executed with the expectation that they would incite retail terrorism. The U.S.-backed Israeli invasion of Lebanon in 1982 is another case, as discussed in Chapter Two. The attack on Libya may also sooner or later inspire terrorist acts, which will serve to mobilise domestic and foreign opinion in support of U.S. plans at home and abroad. If Americans react, as they have, by general hysteria, including fear of travelling to Europe where visitors will be at least one hundred times as safe as they are in any American city, this, too, is a net benefit, for the same reason.

The real reasons for the U.S. attack on Libya have nothing to do with self-defense against "terrorist attacks" on U.S. forces in Beirut in October 1983, as Shimon Peres would have it, or any of the other actions attributed rightly or wrongly to Libya, or "self-defense against future attack" in accord with the remarkable doctrine proclaimed by the Reagan Administration to much domestic acclaim.

Libya's terrorism is a minor irritant, but Qaddafi has stood in the way of U.S. plans in North Africa, the Middle East, and elsewhere: supporting Polisario and anti-U.S. groups in the Sudan, forging a union with Morocco, intervening in Chad,[58] and in general interfering with U.S. efforts to forge a "strategic consensus" in the region and to impose its will elsewhere. These are real crimes, which must be punished.

Furthermore, the Libyan attack had the purpose, and the effect, of preparing opinion at home and abroad for further acts of U.S. violence. The immediate response might be negative, but once absorbed, the level of expectation is heightened and the U.S. can proceed to further escalation if the need arises.

There are two major areas where such escalation is likely. The first is Central America. While the U.S. proxy army has succeeded in its major task of "forcing [the Sandinistas] to divert scarce resources to the war and away from social programs," as explained in a rare moment of candour by Administration officials,[59] it is unlikely that it can "cut out the cancer," to adopt the Nazi-style rhetoric affected by George Shultz and others[60]; hence the threat of successful independent development in terms that might be meaningful to the suffering population of U.S. client states will remain.

Domestic and international pressures prevent the U.S. from attacking directly, as it attacked South Vietnam in 1962 and later all of Indochina; and the more indirect means of terror, while largely successful in El Salvador, may prove inadequate for Nicaragua. It would be natural, then, for the U.S. to move to an arena where it is more likely to prevail: international confrontation.

The U.S. has succeeded in cowing most of its allies into refraining from offering meaningful assistance to Nicaragua, thus largely achieving the goal of compelling the Sandinistas to rely on the Soviet bloc for survival. The Congressional debates over aid are basically a sideshow; a lawless Administration will find ways of funding its terrorist army somehow, whatever Congress legislates. What is important is a different victory: Congressional authorisation for direct CIA involvement and escalation by other means.

The obvious means are threats to Soviet and Cuban shipping. Nicaragua would not be able to respond, but the USSR and Cuba might. If they do attempt to defend their shipping, the U.S. propaganda system can be counted on to react with outrage over this new proof of Communist aggression, allowing the Administration to construct an international crisis in which, it may be assumed, the USSR will back down, so that Nicaragua will be effectively blockaded. If they do not respond, the same result will be achieved. Of course, the world may go up in flames, but that is a minor consideration in comparison with the need to excise the cancer. U.S. and European opinion must be prepared for these eventualities. The bombing of Libya turns the ratchet another notch.

The second area where world opinion must be prepared for possible escalation is the Middle East. The U.S. has blocked political settlement of the Arab-Israeli conflict at least since 1971, as discussed earlier, and it still does. In the situation of military confrontation that results from U.S.-Israeli rejectionism, Israel cannot permit any combination

140

of Arab states to approach its military power, since it will face the threat of destruction.

The Camp David agreements succeeded in excluding the major Arab state, Egypt, from the conflict, thus allowing Israel to expand its steps towards integrating the occupied territories and to attack its northern neighbour. But Syria continues to be a growing threat, and sooner or later Israel will have to act to eliminate it. There is constant war talk in Israel, generally alleging Syrian belligerency and threat but concealing the Israeli intention—indeed, need, as long as a political settlement is averted—to act to eliminate a possible military rival. The U.S. media follow meekly along, as usual.

Meanwhile, the U.S. government surely wants to leave its options open. It would make sense for an Israeli strike against Syria to be accompanied by U.S. bombing, the former presented as a "pre-emptive strike" in "self-defense against future attack," the latter packaged for Western consumption as "self-defense" against Syrian-inspired terrorism. The purpose of direct U.S. participation would be to warn the Soviet Union that a global war will result from any attempt on their part to support their Syrian ally.

European and U.S. opinion must be prepared for such possible moves. The attack on Libya, and the subsequent propaganda campaigns, help set the stage, leaving the U.S. more free to consider these options if are later deemed necessary. Again, the likelihood of a nuclear war is not small, but the U.S. has shown repeatedly that it is prepared to face this danger to achieve its ends in the Middle East, as elsewhere.

The fraudulence and cynicism of the propaganda campaign about "international terrorism" has been exposed to the tiny audiences that can be reached by dissident opinion in the United States, but the campaign itself has been a remarkable public relations achievement. With the mass media committed to serve the needs of the state propaganda system, systematically excluding any commentary that might expose what is unfolding before their eyes and any rational discussion of it, the prospects for future successes continue to be impressive.

This service of the educated classes to wholesale international terrorism contributes to enormous suffering and brutality, and, in the longer term, carries with it serious dangers of superpower confrontation and terminal nuclear war. But such considerations count for little in comparison with the need to ensure that no threat to "stability" and "order" can arise, no challenge to privilege and power.

There is little here to surprise any honest student of history.

Notes

1. *Amnesty International Report—1985* (London, 1985); *Political Killings by Governments* (Amnesty International Report, London, 1983).
2. William Brecher, *The Boston Globe*, April 15, 1986.
3. The U.S. government claims that in Sept. 1980 Nicaragua began to send arms to the guerrillas who were largely mobilised by the Carter-Duarte terrorist war against the population—a mere trickle, even if we accept the documentary evidence provided at face value. The evidence for arms flow from early 1981 is virtually nil (cf. my *Turning the Tide: The U.S. and Latin America* (Black Rose Books, 2nd revised edition, 1987) and the testimony of CIA analyst David MacMichael before the International Court of Justice (World Court); U.N. A/40/907, S/17639, Nov. 19, 1985). It is, of course, assumed without question in the United States that to provide arms to people attempting to defend themselves against a terrorist war launched by the U.S. is criminal, if not proof of an attempt to conquer the hemisphere. The World Court ruled on June 27, 1986, that arms supply might have proceeded "up to the early months of 1981," though further allegations "are not solidly established," and ruled that as a matter of law, such arms supply, even if it existed, would not constitute "armed attack" justifying a U.S. response, as the U.S. government had claimed. It therefore found that U.S. actions "violated the principle [of the U.N. Charter] prohibiting recourse to the threat or use of force" in international affairs, along with other crimes. The response in the U.S. was to ignore the judgement of the Court as irrelevant, while respected advocates

of World Order concluded that the U.S. should not submit to the jurisdiction of the Court, since America "still needs the freedom to protect freedom," as in Nicaragua (Thomas M. Franck, *The New York Times*, July 17, 1986). *Contra* lobbyist Robert Leiken of the Carnegie Endowment for International Peace "blamed the court, which he said suffers from the 'increasing perception' of having close ties to the Soviet Union"— ties that have suddenly emerged since the same Court ruled in favour of the U.S. in the case of Iran in 1980 (Jonathan Karp, *The Washington Post*, June 28, 1986). All of this is, once again, the reaction one would expect in a major centre of international terrorism.

4. Editorial, *The Washington Post* (*The Manchester Guardian Weekly*, Feb. 22, 1981); Alan Riding, *The New York Times*, Sept. 27, 1981. See *Turning the Tide, op. cit.*, for references not given here or below.

5. Ambrose Evans-Pritchard, *The Spectator*, May 10, 1986; with the task of decapitation largely accomplished, he continues, the numbers of corpses "are down and the bodies are dropped discreetly at night into the middle of Lake Ilopango and only rarely wash up onto the shore to remind bathers that the repression is still going on." Editorials, *The New Republic*, April 2, 1984, April 7, 1986. On recent atrocities, see Americas Watch, *Settling Into Routine* (May 1986), reporting that political killings and disappearances—ninety percent at the hands of Duarte's armed forces—continue at well over four a day, a real improvement in this leading terrorist state, along with numerous other government atrocities.

6. Chris Krueger and Kjell Enge, *Security and Development Conditions in the Guatemalan Highlands* (Washington Office on Latin America, 1985); Alan Nairn, "The Guatemala Connection," *The Progressive*, May, Sept. 1986. On the Israeli connection, in Central America and elsewhere, see now Benjamin Beit-Hallahmi, *From Manila to Managua: Israel's World War* (Pantheon, forthcoming).

7. Herman and Brodhead, *Demonstration Elections* (South End, 1984). They define this concept to refer to a device of foreign intervention in which elections are "organized and staged by a foreign power primarily to pacify a restive home population," discussing several other examples as well and showing in detail that they are no less farcical than elections held under Soviet authority. Their term "demonstration elections" was borrowed and radically misused with reference to Nicaragua by Robert

Leiken (*The New York Review*, Dec. 5, 1985) as part of his campaign in support of the terrorist proxy army. See Brodhead and Herman's letter, published after half a year's delay along with others by British Parliamentary observers (June 26, 1986), and Leiken's response, tacitly conceding the accuracy of their critique (by evasion) while claiming that they designed their concept "as a way of focusing attention on Western imperialism while diverting it from Soviet imperialism... in line with their apparent belief that there is only one superpower villain"; this is the standard reflex of apologists for state terror whose deceit is exposed, in this case requiring the suppression of Brodhead and Herman's harsh critique of elections in Poland along with much else. The remainder of Leiken's responses and his articles themselves maintain a comparable level of integrity and merit careful reading for those interested in the workings of the U.S. ideological system. See particularly the critique by Alexander Cockburn (*The Nation*, Dec. 29, 1985, May 10, 1986) and Leiken's evasive attempt to respond (*The New York Review of Books*, June 26); also my introduction to Morris Morley and James Petras, *The Reagan Administration and Nicaragua* (Pamphlet Series, Institute for Media Analysis, New York), forthcoming.

8. Council on Hemispheric Affairs, *Washington Report on the Hemisphere*, April 16, 1986. From Cerezo's inauguration in January, through June, the number of murders is estimated at seven hundred, a rise of ten percent over the preceding year; how many are political, or what the actual numbers are, is unknown (Edward Cody, *The Washington Post*, July 6, 1986). Alan Nairn and Jean-Marie Simon estimate political killings at more than sixty a month, victims of "an efficient system of political terrorism" run by the Guatemalan military using such devices as a "computer file on journalists, students, leaders, people of the left, politicians and so on"—a system given to them by Israel, though this fact, and the Israeli connection in general, is unmentioned, and is generally unmentionable in this journal (*The New Republic*, June 30, 1986). "Guatemala's bureaucracy of death appears more comfortably entrenched than at any time since the mid-1960s," they conclude, noting that President "Cerezo has yet to denounce a single army killing" and that "his interior minister said that political murders are no longer a problem"—a stance that is understandable, or they, too, will disappear in this terrorist client state.

9. John Haiman and Anna Meigs, "Khaddafy: Man and Myth,"*Africa Events*, Feb. 1986.

10. See my *Turning the Tide, op. cit.*, for an ample selection; also Chapter Two, notes 17, 44, and references cited above.

11. Michael Ledeen, *The National Interest*, Spring 1986. See note 4 and text.

12. Editorial, *The New York Times*, April 20, 1985; *The Washington Post*, Jan. 11, 1986; Rabin, *The Boston Globe*, Jan. 25, 1986; *El Pais* (Madrid), April 25, 1986.

13. E.J. Dionne, "Syria Terror Link Cited by Italian," June 25, 1986; *The Times* editors are surely aware that the remainder of the U.S. government case that they applauded has collapsed, as we shall see directly.

14. *The New York Times*, June 27, 1985; *The Christian Science Monitor*, March 25, 1986. Cuban mercenaries fighting with the U.S. proxy army attacking Nicaragua allege that they were trained at a paramilitary base in Florida; Stephen Kinzer, *The New York Times*, June 26, 1986. The U.S. government has, however, arrested plotters attempting to overthrow the dictatorship of Suriname in New Orleans (described by the U.S. attorney as "a 'jumping-off point' for mercenaries seeking to become involved in South and Central America"), charging them with violation of the U.S. Neutrality Act (*The Christian Science Monitor*, July 30, 1986), just as it had previously blocked efforts to overthrow the murderous Duvalier regime it supported in Haiti, thus demonstrating its firm commitment to the Rule of Law.

15. Bob Woodward and Charles R. Babcock, *The Washington Post*, May 12.

16. Ihsan Hijazi, *The New York Times*, April 20, 1986. The careful reader of *The Times* will find, buried in a report from Athens by Henry Kamm (May 29, 1986), a denunciation of terrorism by Syrian President Assad, specifically the killing of 144 Syrians in a "major terrorist action," presumably referring to the bombs on Syrian buses.

17. Philip Shenon, *The New York Times*, May 14, 1985; Lou Cannon, Bob Woodward, *et al.*, *The Washington Post*, April 28, 1986.

18. *The New Republic*, Jan. 20, 1986; Edwin Meese, AP, April 4, 1986; see Chapter Two.

19. Frank Greve, *The Philadelphia Inquirer*, May 18, 1986.

20. Nef, *Middle East International* (London), April 4, 1986; Johnson, *The Sunday Telegraph* (London), June 1, 1986. Johnson's comments reflect the typical stance of this highly respected apologist for state terrorism. Thus in an Israeli-organised propaganda

conference on terrorism in Washington (see the preface, note 15), he praised Israel for taking "drastic measures" to fight "the terrorist cancer" as in its 1982 invasion of Lebanon: "The truth is, by having the moral and physical courage to violate a so-called sovereign frontier, and by placing the moral law above the formalities of state rights, Israel was able for the first time to strike at the heart of the cancer, to arrest its growth and to send it into headlong retreat" (Wolf Blitzer, *The Jerusalem Post*, June 29, 1984)—the precise opposite of Israel's intent, as discussed in Chapter Two.

21. Edward Haley, *Qaddafi and the United States Since 1969* (Praeger, 1984), p. 271f.

22. Larry Speakes, national TV, 7:30 p.m., April 14; *The New York Times*, April 16; AP, April 14; *The New York Times*, April 15; Lewis, *The New York Times*, April 17; Bernard Weinraub, *The New York Times*, April 15, 1986; Jeff Sallot, *The Globe & Mail* (Toronto), April 24, 1986. As noted earlier, the World Court has rejected the U.S. contention (with respect to El Salvador, not, say, Afghanistan, Angola, or Cambodia) that arms flow to guerrillas constitutes "armed attack." See note 3.

23. Haley, *Qaddafi and the U.S. Since 1969, op. cit.*, pp. 8, 264.

24. *The New Statesman*, Aug. 16, 1985.

25. See *The Financial Times*, p. 210; Haley, *op. cit.*, who makes a praiseworthy effort to take the comedy seriously.

26. "The Central Intelligence Agency, barred from providing military aid to Nicaragua rebels, secretly funneled several million dollars to the rebels for political projects over the past year, U.S. government officials say," also allowing "the CIA to maintain a strong influence over the rebel movement, even though a Congressional ban existed from October 1984 through September 1985, prohibiting the agency from spending money 'which would have the effect of supporting, directly or indirectly, military or paramilitary operations in Nicaragua,' the officials said." One purpose of what U.S. officials described as "a major program" was to "create the aura that [the *contras*] are an actual political entity among our allies in Europe." Congressman Sam Gejdenson stated, "We suspected that the CIA had never really withdrawn from the scene, but the extent of the agency's direct involvement in the Contra war may astound even the most jaded observer." UNO (*contra*) documents obtained by AP "show much of UNO's political money going to military organizations allied with the umbrella group" established by

the U.S., while some of the funds were used to pay off Honduran and Costa Rican officials "to enable the rebels to operate in those countries." Much of the money was funnelled through a London-based bank in the Bahamas. AP, April 14; *The Boston Globe*, April 14, 1986. The disclosures passed with no comment at the time, and little afterwards. Subsequently, *The Miami Herald* reported that more than $2 million of the $27 million provided by Congress for "humanitarian assistance" was used to pay Honduran officers "to turn a blind eye to illegal contra activities on Honduran soil" (editorial, *The Boston Globe*, May 13, 1986), along with much evidence of corruption that received some limited notice, to no effect.

27. AP, March 27, 1986, citing *El Pais* (Madrid).

28. R.C. Longworth, *The Chicago Tribune*, March 30, 1986.

29. Richard Higgins, *The Boston Globe*, March 25, 1986.

30. Fred Kaplan, *The Boston Globe*, March 26, 1986.

31. *The London Sunday Times*, April 6, 1986.

32. Cockburn, *The Wall St. Journal*, April 17; also *The Nation*, April 26, 1986. Lelyveld, *The New York Times*, April 18, 1986.

33. Another injured black GI died several months later.

34. *The New York Times*, April 16, 1986.

35. *The New York Times*, April 18, 1986; the *Times* report states that at 7 p.m. F-111s bombed military targets "near Benghazi" and "near Tripoli," and that at 7:06 p.m. they bombed "the Tripoli military airport, the final target." In fact, as the editors knew, the F-111s bombed a residential neighbourhood in Tripoli.

36. AP, April 14, 1986.

37. James M. Markham, *The New York Times*, April 25, 1986.

38. *Der Spiegel*, April 21, 1986; the front cover features the phrase "Terror Against Terror," a well-known Gestapo slogan, presumably not selected by accident. See also Norman Birnbaum's article, same issue.

39. Text of interview provided by an American journalist with *Stars and Stripes* in Germany.

40. See, for example, James M. Markham, *The New York Times*, May 31, citing a "West Berlin police investigoator" who "said he believed that the Libyan Embassy in East Berlin 'conceived' the attack"—well short of the "certainties" asserted earlier—and cites Manfred Ganschow, but not on his denial of any evidence; or Robert Suro, *The New York Times*, July 3, on possible involvement of Syria and the Abu Nidal anti-Arafat

terrorists in the discothèque bombing, referring to "evidence that *reportedly* showed" Libyan involvement (my emphasis); or Bernard Weinraub, *The New York Times*, June 9, referring to possible Syrian involvement and what Administration officials "said" they knew about Libyan intercepts.

41.   Bakhash, *The New York Review of Books*, Aug. 14, 1986.

42.   *The Christian Science Monitor*, April 22, 1986; see Chapter One, at note 3.

43.   *The Globe & Mail* (Toronto), editorials, March 28, 18, 5, 1986, referring specifically to Nicaragua.

44.   See AP, *The International Herald Tribune*, May 6, for extensive discussion; *The New York Times*, May 6, 1986, a briefer mention, and the text of the statement against terrorism.

45.   AP, April 14; survey of world press reaction, AP, April 15; survey of U.S. editorial reaction, April 16; editorial, *The New York Times*, April 15, 1986; Peres, *The New York Times*, April 16.

46.   After the Libya bombing, there were numerous references to American punitive expeditions against the Barbary pirates; no one seems to have gone back a few steps further in history to describe the days when "New York had become a thieve's [*sic*] market where pirates disposed of loot taken on the high seas," as piracy enriched the American colonies, like the British before them (Nathan Miller, *The Founding Finaglers*, David McKay, 1976, pp. 25-26). Piracy was not a Libyan invention, courageously suppressed by American guardians of order.

47.   AP, April 21, *The New York Times*, April 20; survey of religious reactions, AP, April 17; also April 19, reporting a news conference of fourteen religious and community groups in Seattle condemning the bombing in contrast to support for it by the Western Washington Rabbinic Board; Nye, *The Boston Globe*, April 16; Rostow, *The New York Times*, April 27.

48.   Charles Glass, *The Spectator* (London), May 3, 1986. A facsimile of the original was submitted to the American press as a letter to the editor, but was not published. The text was published by Alexander Cockburn (*In These Times*, July 23, 1986), with a suggestion that since President and Mrs. Reagan "are fond of reading out messages from small children, they might care to deliver this one on the next appropriate occasion."

49.   *Dissent*, Summer 1986. Observing on the scene, Ramsey Clark concluded from the pattern of bombing that the well-to-do suburb where the worst civilian casualties were suffered must have been a specific target; *The Nation*, July 5, 1986. The

question is irrelevant to the issue of terrorism, as anyone who is not a moral idiot will understand at once (Clark, of course, does not suggest otherwise).

50. *The new Republic*, Sept. 6, 1982; for other samples of the opinions of this respected figure, see Chapters One and Two, above, and Noam Chomsky, *The Fateful Triangle: Israel, the United States, and the Palestinians* (Black Rose Books, 1984).

51. *The Washington Post Weekly*, Aug. 4, 1986.

52. Ignatius, *The Washington Post Weekly*, July 28, 1986.

53. *The Christian Science Monitor*, June 25, July 16, 1986.

54. *The Economist* (London), July 26, 1986; *The Christian Science Monitor*, July 24, 1986.

55. One must take these numbers with a grain of salt, given the ideological considerations that enter into defining an act as "terrorist." Thus bombing of abortion clinics was excluded from the category of "terrorism" at one time, and may still be. According to columnist Cal Thomas of the Moral Majority, there were three hundred bombings "on property where abortions are performed" from 1982 through late 1984, which he thinks are "probably not a good idea... tactically, as well as politically"—though they are apparently just fine "morally"; *The Boston Globe*, Nov. 30, 1984.

56. AP, *The Globe & Mail* (Toronto), July 4, 1986; Stephen Engelberg, "Official Says F.B.I. Has Suspects in Blasts Laid to Extremist Jews," *The New York Times*, July 17, 1985; *The Washington Post*, Peyman Pejman, July 5, 17.

57. *The New Republic*, Jan. 20, 1986; Edwin Meese, AP, April 4, 1986; see Chapter Two. Recall that the record of Zionist terrorism against civilians goes back many years, long before the establishment of the state of Israel; see my *Fateful Triangle, op. cit.*, p. 164f.

58. The first Libyan intervention followed the dispatch of French Foreign Legion forces, advisers, and aircraft (Haley, *op. cit.*, p. 98), but French intervention in Africa is legitimate, indeed laudable; as *Business Week* commented cheerily, French forces help "keep West Africa safe for French, American, and other foreign oilmen" (Aug. 10, 1981) and perform similar services elsewhere.

59. Julia Preston, *The Boston Globe*, Feb. 9, 1986.

60. Speaking at Kansas State University, Shultz "drew sustained applause when he said, 'Nicaragua is a cancer, and we must cut it out'." He also explained that "negotiations are a euphemism for capitulation if the shadow of power is not cast across the bargaining table," another familiar thought.

CHAPTER FOUR
The U.S. Role
in the Middle East

The following letter of recommendation for me was sent
to a small journal in England, *Index on Censorship*, in which
I had published a brief article of about three thousand words:

Dear Dan:

Forgive me for writing to you again in your capacity
as a Director and Member of the Editorial Board of *Index
on Censorship*, but I can't resist. In the latest issue which
I have, July/August 1986, there appears a truly astonishing
article, beginning on p. 2 and continuing at great length.
This article is an attack on the United States, the United
States Government, and the United States press by Noam
Chomsky.

You probably know about Chomsky: he is a fanatical
defender of the PLO who has set new standards for intellectual dishonesty and personal vindictiveness in his
writings about the Middle East. There really isn't anyone
left in the U.S.—without regard to politics—who takes
Chomsky seriously in view of his astonishing record. I
therefore find it inexplicable that he is given fully three
pages to go on with his attack on one of the freest presses
in the world. Clearly giving him this much space lends
a certain respectability to his disreputable efforts. Can it
be that your editors simply do not know who Chomsky
is and are unfamiliar with his record? Can it be that,

fully familiar with him, they nevertheless decided to give him this platform? If so, why?

I hope this letter finds you and your family well, and send you best regards from my wife.

(Signed "Elliott," that is, Elliott Abrams, Assistant Secretary of State for Inter-American Affairs, July 29, 1986, on official State Department stationery.)

I cite this letter for two reasons. One, because I naturally treasure it, just as I treasure, for precisely the same reasons, the efforts of Soviet advisers in the Third World to have my books banned (as they are in the USSR) and the rejection of my only visa application to Eastern Europe; the reactions of the commissars often indicate that one is on the right course. But beyond that, the letter gives a revealing (and rather typical) insight into the mentality of the Reagan Administration and also of the Israeli lobby—I should mention that Abrams' letter was only one part of a barrage launched against the journal for daring to publish remarks on the U.S. and Israel that were deemed improper, all in a style familiar from the annals of Stalinism.[1]

Let me put aside the remarkable lack of a sense of irony; recall that this is a journal devoted to *censorship*, and it is now under attack because it permitted expression of fact and analysis not to the taste of the commissars. What the letter reveals is the totalitarian streak in the mentality of leading figures in the Reagan Administration: not even the tiniest opening must be allowed to unacceptable thought. The letter is also typical of the style that has been the hallmark of this Administration. I do not want to suggest that it is outside the spectrum of American politics; unfortunately, it is not. But in its practices, its style, and its commitments, the Reagan Administration does represent an extreme position within this spectrum, an extreme of reactionary jingoism— which has misappropriated the honourable term "conservative"—marked by fanatic lying, lawlessness, enhancement of state power and violence, attacks on personal freedom and civil liberties. These developments are all ominous in character and are important for the future of American politics and

152

society, hence for the Middle East, and for the world, given the awesome scale of American power.

These features of the Reagan Administration have not gone unnoticed, and they have naturally aroused concern among genuine conservatives in the United States—of whom, incidentally, there are very few in government or the media— and abroad. A few years ago, David Watt, Director of the Royal Institute of International Affairs in London, writing in the Establishment journal *Foreign Affairs*, commented on

> the chasm that lies between current American perceptions of the world and the world's perception of America... with the possible exceptions of the Israelis, the South Africans, President Marcos of the Philippines and a few right-wing governments in Central and South America, [most of the world believes] that the Reagan administration has vastly overreacted to the Soviet threat, thereby distorting the American (and hence the world) economy, quickening the arms race, warping its own judgment about events in the Third World, and further debasing the language of international intercourse with feverish rhetoric.

He adds that "it is in my experience almost impossible to convey even to the most experienced Americans just how deeply rooted and widely spread the critical view has become"—also an important fact. As if to confirm this judgement, in a companion article on the current international scene in *Foreign Affairs*, editor William Bundy writes that with regard to the "degree of threat from the Soviet Union... the Reagan administration's broad view seems to this observer nearer to reality than the often excessively sanguine and parochial stated positions of other major nations."[2]

Watt, in fact, exaggerates the "chasm." European elites are not that removed from Reaganite hysteria, and the "exceptions" go beyond those he mentioned, particularly France, where many Paris intellectuals have adopted Reaganite fanaticism as their current fad. Furthermore, as Bundy's comment indicates, Watt is describing elite opinion in the U.S. well beyond the Reagan Administration. He is describing the extreme version of a general elite reaction to the problems caused by the Vietnam war, including the harm caused to the U.S. economy and the benefits to America's industrial rivals, and the breakdown of discipline both in the Third World and at home. These factors require stern state action and thus an appeal to the Russian threat, which is regularly invoked in such situations. But Watt's essential point is accurate enough.

The isolation of the U.S. has since increased, as revealed, for example, by votes in the United Nations on a wide range of issues. In the fall of 1986, the General Assembly voted 124 to 1 in favour of a South Atlantic zone of peace and 94 to 3 calling on the U.S. to comply with the World Court ruling ordering a cessation of U.S. aggression against Nicaragua; in the latter case, the U.S. was joined by two client states, El Salvador (which is "independent" in the sense in which Poland is independent of the USSR) and Israel (which has turned itself into an armed mercenary of the United States). U.S. isolation on Middle East votes is notorious. In general, in the 1980s (through 1985) the U.S. resorted to twenty-seven vetoes in the Security Council, as compared to fifteen in the earlier history of the U.N. (all since 1966) and four vetoes for the USSR in the 1980s.[3]

The reaction to all of this in the United States, incidentally, is quite interesting. In the early days of the U.N., when it was firmly under U.S. control and could be used for Cold War purposes, the general attitude towards the organisation was highly favourable and there was much earnest debate over what caused the USSR, which was then almost isolated, to be so negative; perhaps this was a result of the practice of using swaddling clothes for infants, which reinforced "negativism," some suggested. As U.S. global dominance declined from its quite phenomenal post-war peak (which probably had no parallel in history) and the relative independence of U.N. members increased, American attitudes became more critical, and by now are extremely hostile. We no longer read disquisitions on the curious negativism of the Russians, but rather on the equally curious fact that the world is out of step, as *New York Times* U.N. correspondent Richard Bernstein thoughtfully explains.[4]

Opinion polls in Europe show similar results. A recent classified USIA poll shows that outside of France, European opinion trusts Mikhail Gorbachev on arms control far more than Reagan, by four to one in England and seven to one in Germany.[5]

I should add that all of this, and much more evidence like it, is virtually concealed in the U.S. None of what I have just mentioned has been reported in *The New York Times*, for example.

The international isolation is of little concern to the Reagan Administration. They have shown a shrewd understanding of the efficacy of violence and intimidation. Like some of their predecessors and models elsewhere in the world, they are well aware that cheap victories over weak and defenseless enemies will arouse jingoist sentiments and popular enthusiasm at home, if the population can be properly terrified by grave threats to its existence—Hitler's appeals to the encirclement of Germany by hostile states bent on its destruction, the Czech "dagger pointed at the heart of Germany," and the aggressiveness and terror of the Czechs and the Poles come to mind as obvious examples. The Reaganites understand very well what the American satirist H.L. Mencken called "the whole aim of practical politics": "to keep the public alarmed (and hence clamorous to be led to safety) by menacing it with an endless series of hobgoblins, all of them imaginary."

As for the rest of the world, U.S. cultural hegemony is sufficiently great that doctrines contrived for domestic purposes will be adopted or taken seriously, however ludicrous they may be; and if not, the threat of escalated violence if U.S. allies prove intransigent, and its potential costs to them, always remains credible and has been effectively exploited.

The propaganda campaign around international terrorism is one example of the skillful use of these techniques, both at home and abroad. Policy-makers of the Reagan Administration know that liberal elements in Congress and the media can easily be cowed by the charge that they are soft and not militant enough in the face of whatever hobgoblin happens to be the monster of the day, and hence will line up obediently in the "crusade against terrorism."

They also understand that the overwhelming resources of violence at their command allow utter disdain for world opinion. In fact, they regularly exploit concerns over their violence, as in the Tokyo summit after the Libya bombings, when the Reaganites rallied Western elites by warning them that unless they fell in line, there is no telling what the "crazy Americans" might do next, a warning presented in an Administration position paper at the summit.

The disdainful attitude towards Congress is revealed at every turn. For example, in the military authorisation bill, both houses of Congress insisted on wording that called upon the executive to comply with SALT II, in the interest of national security. A few weeks later, the Administration announced that it was proceeding to exceed the SALT II limits. An Administration spokesman explained that "Congress is out of town and the summit in Iceland is past. [Gorbachev] is not expected to come here for some time. So what's holding us back?"[6] In other words, the cop is looking the other way, so why not rob the store? In actual fact, Congress has been out of town even when it is in town, as the Administration knows very well, and it has not proven too difficult for a gang of street toughs to ride roughshod over the generally pathetic opposition.

The attitude towards the public is revealed by what one Reagan official called "a vast psychological warfare operation" designed to set the agenda for debate over Nicaragua—a disinformation campaign called (naturally) "Operation Truth"; Goebbels and Stalin would have been amused.[7]

Disinformation has been an Administration speciality since the early days, though the media and Congress always profess to be shocked when a new example is exposed—the summer 1986 disinformation campaign concerning Libya, for example. In this particular instance, the display of outrage necessitated a slight case of amnesia; as early as August 1981, *Newsweek* had reported a government "disinformation program designed to embarrass Qaddafi and his government" along with assorted acts of U.S. terrorism within Libya to try to "demonstrate that Qaddafi was opposed by an indigenous political force." There have also been extensive disinformation campaigns, quite successful thanks to media cooperation, on the arms race and numerous other matters.[8]

We derive further insights from current revelations about the sophisticated programme to evade Congressional restrictions on military aid to the terrorist proxy army attacking Nicaragua—or the "resistance," as it is termed by government disinformation and the loyal press, a "resistance" organised by the Hemispheric Enforcer to attack Nicaragua from bases established outside its borders (the term "proxy army," in contrast, is used in internal White House documents, and its terrorism is also not concealed in secret reports).

To mention one illustration of the careful planning that lies behind the terrorist operations, consider the decision of the Reagan Administration to sell (probably quite useless) AWACs to Saudi Arabia in 1981. This was a politically unpopular move, and it was not clear at the time why the Administration was so determined to pursue it. The reasons have now become rather clear. The Reagan planners evidently anticipated potential difficulties in funding their proxy army, and when Congress, responding to public pressure, sought two years later to limit the terrorist war against Nicaragua, Saudi Arabia was called upon to repay its debt and to fund shipments of arms to the *contras*, apparently Soviet arms that had been captured during the U.S.-backed Israeli aggression in Lebanon.[9]

These are the machinations of sophisticated international terrorists with a global vision. Now that these machinations have finally surpassed the point where they could be suppressed, the partial exposures will elicit the pretense that the Reagan policy-makers are incompetent bunglers; the invariable elite response to failure of state plans is to focus attention on alleged personal inadequacies, so as to avert the threat that the public will come to understand the systematic nature of policy, the general support for it within elite circles (tactics aside), and the institutional roots of these commitments. But no one should be deluded into believing that we are witnessing the operations of fools and bunglers; their achievements in organising efficient international terrorism are impressive, from the Middle East to Central America, and beyond.

Another crucial fact hardly likely to be emphasised by articulate opinion should be kept in mind: the current scandals are a great tribute to the popular movements begun in the 1960s, which forced the state to resort to clandestine operations for its terrorism and violence, operations so complex that finally they could not be entirely kept from public view. Had the public continued to be apathetic and quiescent, Reagan could have emulated the practices of John F. Kennedy when he simply sent the U.S. Air Force to carry out large-scale bombing and defoliation missions in Vietnam in 1961-62, or Lyndon Johnson when he openly escalated the aggression against South Vietnam by land and air, extended it to the north, and sent twenty-three thousand Marines to the Dominican Republic to avert the threat of democracy there. This all occurred in early 1965, with very little protest. Clandestine operations carry the risk of exposure, and of undermining the rhetorical pose of the government (for example, "combatting terrorism"). This may inhibit the terrorist commanders, for a time at least.

These facts serve to show that even in a generally depoliticised society like the United States, with no political parties or major media outside the narrow business-based elite consensus, significant public action is quite possible and may influence policy, though indirectly, as it did in the Vietnam years. These are important facts to bear in mind in connection with the Middle East as well.

One central institution of the U.S.-organised international terror network is the World Anti-Communist League, a collection of Nazis, fanatic anti-Semites, death-squad assassins, and some of the worst killers and thugs around the world, mobilised by the Reagan Administration into an effective network of murderers and torturers, worldwide in scope. The League attracted some attention in the course of the Hasenfus affair in Nicaragua.

The New York Times, as usual reporting government propaganda as fact, claimed that the League had been purged of its more nefarious elements when General Singlaub took it over in the 1980s. This is untrue. The World Anti-Communist League had just then completed its annual conference in Europe (which was not reported in the media in the United

States, to my knowledge). The leading Nazis were present and were given respectful applause when their leaders— Nazi killers from the days of Hitler—mounted the podium to address the audience. The Latin-American death-squad leaders, allegedly expelled in 1984, reappeared at once at 1984-85 conferences sponsored by the U.S. affiliate—which is, incidentally, a tax-exempt "educational" organisation.

The League continues to include Nazis, assorted racists, and killers from around the world. It is supported by the U.S. and several of its client states, particularly Taiwan and South Korea, but also reportedly by Syria and other Arab states, and its workings are concealed by the Israeli lobby in the United States. In the introduction to their recent book on the League, Scott Anderson and John Anderson comment that the Anti-Defamation League of B'nai Brith, a leading component of the domestic Israeli lobby, refused to provide them with information on this notorious collection of anti-Semites, who now serve a useful purpose within the Reaganite international terror network that they generally support. [10]

All of this, and much more, reveals a sophisticated understanding of how to conduct international terrorism, on a scale with few historical precedents.

The sordid record of the World Anti-Communist League should remind us that while Reaganite thuggery is unusual, it is not unique in U.S. history. Immediately after World War II, the U.S. turned to the task of suppressing the anti-fascist resistance throughout much of the world, often in favour of fascists and collaborators. One component of this global programme was the recruitment of Nazi gangsters such as Klaus Barbie, "the Butcher of Lyons," who had been responsible for horrendous atrocities in France and was duly placed in charge of spying on the French for American intelligence. A far more important example was Reinhard Gehlen, who had been in charge of Hitler's East European intelligence operations and was quickly assigned the same tasks under the CIA, in West German intelligence. His organisation was responsible for U.S. support for military actions within the USSR and Eastern Europe, in conjunction with armies that had been encouraged by Hitler. These operations were run out of George Kennan's office in the State Department, according to John Loftus, who investigated these matters for the U.S. Justice Department.

Later, when many of these useful folk could no longer be protected in Europe, the U.S. authorities brought them to the United States or to Latin America with the aid of the Vatican and fascist priests. They have continued to serve U.S. government interests, training torturers in methods devised by the Gestapo, helping establish the neo-Nazi national security states in Latin America and the Central American death squad apparatus within the framework of the U.S.-trained security forces, and so on.[11]

We will understand very little about the world if we neglect the relevant historical context, which is naturally ignored or suppressed in official doctrine.

The same is true when we turn directly to the Middle East. Consider U.S. relations with Iran, which are now in the news but with the historical context largely excised — as is usually the case when it teaches inconvenient lessons. The Reagan Administration argues that the arms shipments to Iran via an Israeli connection are part of an effort to establish contacts with "moderate" elements in Iran. There is a sense in which this claim is doubtless true; namely, if we depart from English and enter the domain of standard Orwellian Newspeak, in which the term "moderate" is a euphemism for elements that are properly obedient to U.S. orders and demands; it is counterposed to "radical," a term that refers to those who do not follow orders properly. Notice that the terminology has nothing to do with the commitment to violence and terror of these groups, or even their social and political goals, apart from the crucial defining feature; thus the mass murderer Suharto in Indonesia is a respected "moderate," but a peasant self-help group organised by the Church in El Salvador is "radical," and must be extirpated by Pol Pot-style terror conducted by the U.S. mercenary forces.

In Iran, the U.S. restored "moderates" to power with a CIA coup in 1954, in what *The New York Times* (August 6, 1954) described as an "object lesson" to "underdeveloped countries with rich resources," an "object lesson in the cost that must be paid by one of their number which goes berserk with fanatical nationalism" and tries to take control of their own resources—not understanding that those resources really belong to the United States—thus becoming "radical."

Iran remained "moderate" until the fall of the Shah in 1979. It meanwhile compiled one of the worst human rights records in the world, Amnesty International and other human rights groups regularly documented, but this did not affect the classification of the Shah as a "moderate" or the applause for him among U.S. elites. The Shah was supported by the Carter Administration to the very end of his bloody rule. The U.S. then apparently looked into the possibility of a military coup, but without success. Since that time, a flow of arms to Iran has been maintained, in part via Israel, which had very close relations with the Shah and his military.

Notice that very much the same was true in the case of Somoza in Nicaragua, who fell at about the same time. The Carter Administration also backed him until the end, with Israel providing the arms, surely with tacit U.S. backing, while he was killing tens of thousands in a last paroxysm of fury. Carter attempted to impose the rule of the National Guard when Somoza could no longer be maintained. Shortly after, remnants of the Guard were re-established in Honduras and Costa Rica with the aid of U.S. proxies such as Argentina (then under the neo-Nazi generals, and thus a useful "moderate" client state), and were then taken over directly by the U.S. and organised as a terrorist proxy army dedicated to preventing social reform in Nicaragua.

Meanwhile, U.S. elites underwent a magical conversion; they became profoundly concerned, for the first time, with human rights and "democracy" (another Orwellism, referring to guaranteed rule by the military and business-based elements linked to U.S. corporations) in Nicaragua and Iran, a sudden moral awakening that would be regarded with the contempt it richly merits in societies less indoctrinated than the United States.

Returning to Iran, according to Israel's ambassador to the U.S., Moshe Arens, in October 1982, Israel's supply of arms to Iran after the fall of the Shah was carried out "in coordination with the U.S. government... at almost the

161

highest of levels." The objective "was to see if we could not find some areas of contact with the Iranian military, to bring down the Khomeini regime," or at least "to make contact with some military officers who some day might be in a position of power in Iran." Yaakov Nimrodi, the Israeli arms salesman who was military attaché in the Israeli embassy in Iran under the Shah, described this plan over the BBC in 1982. Former Israeli ambassador to Iran Uri Lubrani of the Labour Party added further details, in the same programme:

> I very strongly believe that Tehran can be taken over by a very relatively small force, determined, ruthless, cruel. I mean the men who would lead that force will have to be emotionally geared to the possibility that they'd have to kill ten thousand people.

In short, these men would be "moderates," in the technical sense.

The same ideas were reiterated by David Kimche, head of Israel's Foreign Office and former deputy director of the Mossad. Kimche and Nimrodi are now identified in the media as among those who initiated the current programme of U.S. military aid to Iran via Israel in connection with U.S. hostages and the "search for moderates." The publicised views of the Israelis concerned with these programmes— long before there were any hostages—are suppressed, however. At the same time—early 1982—these plans were generally endorsed, with varying degrees of scepticism as to the feasibility, by Richard Helms (ex-director of the CIA and formerly ambassador to Iran), Robert Komer (a leading candidate for war crimes trials in the late 1960s and a high Pentagon official under Carter, one of the architects of the Rapid Deployment Force which, he suggested, could be used to support "moderates" after a military coup), and others.[12] All this, too, is now suppressed, needless to say.

The same facts were also reported more recently, though they were ignored, well before the scandals erupted; for example, by Israeli senior foreign ministry spokesman Avi Pazner, who confirmed in an interview that in 1982 Israel had sent Iran military supplies with he approval of the U.S., including spare parts for U.S.-made jet fighters. [13]

The arms flow to Iran through Israel (and probably other avenues) has very likely continued at a level sufficient to keep contacts with the proper elements of the Iranian military, though the U.S. is opposed to sending arms at a level that might enable Iran to win the Iran-Iraq war, which would be a disaster for U.S. policy. Thus the U.S. blocked a major arms deal with Israel in April 1986, arresting an Israeli ex-general, among others. [14]

None of this is a discovery of late 1986, as these earlier references indicate. In 1982, a front-page story by current *New York Times* editor Leslie Gelb reported that half of the arms to Iran were "being supplied or arranged by Israel"—surely with U.S. knowledge and at least tacit authorisation—"and the rest by free-lance arms merchants, some of whom may also have connections with Israeli intelligence," while the CIA was carrying out covert actions against the Khomeini regime from its bases in eastern Turkey. [15] And Arens' disclosures were prominently reported in *The Boston Globe* on successive days, among other cases.

More recently, well before the "scandals," additional information repeatedly appeared. Thus in May 1986, Patrick Seale reported that "Israeli and European arms dealers are rushing war supplies to Iran," as Israel now dispenses with "the usual roundabout arms routes"; "for example, a ship now at sea, carrying more than 25,000 tonnes of Israeli artillery, ammunition, gun barrels, aircraft parts and other war supplies" was ordered to proceed directly to Iran instead of transhipping through Zaire. [16] It is hard to take very seriously the current show of surprise on these matters.

Note again the continuing similarity between U.S. policy towards Iran and towards Nicaragua. There, too, it is difficult to take seriously the current show of surprise over the fact that the Reagan Administration has been actively engaged in arranging military support for its proxy army—circumventing Congressional legislation, not to speak of the World Court ruling and laws going back to the eighteenth-century Neutrality Act.

We can learn more about these matters by attending to recent history. Notice first that the pattern of arms sales to Iran is a classic one, another crucial fact scrupulously evaded in current commentary. For example, relations between the U.S. and Indonesia became bitterly hostile thirty years ago, so much so that the CIA sponsored a failed invasion and coup attempt in Indonesia in 1958. During the period of hostility, the U.S. continued to provide arms to the Sukarno regime. In late 1965, the pro-American General Suharto carried out a military coup, leading to the slaughter of several hundred thousand people, mostly landless peasants, and the destruction of the only mass-based political organisation in Indonesia, the Indonesian Communist Party. Indonesia was thus restored to the Free World, opened to robbery and exploitation by U.S., Canadian, European, and Japanese corporations, impeded only by the rapacity of the ruling generals, who imposed a corrupt and brutal dictatorship.

These developments were warmly welcomed by enlightened opinion in the West, and regarded as a vindication of U.S. aggression against South Vietnam (called "defense of South Vietnam" within the propaganda system), which provided a "shield" that encouraged the generals to carry out the necessary purge of their society.

In Senate testimony after the slaughter, Defense Secretary McNamara was asked to explain the supply of arms to Indonesia during the period of intense hostility between the two countries. He was asked whether this arms supply had "paid dividends," and he agreed that it had—some seven hundred thousand dividends, at that point, according to his Indonesian friends. A Congressional report held that training and maintaining communication with military officers paid "enormous dividends" in overthrowing Sukarno.

Similarly, according to Pentagon sources, "United States military influence on local commanders was widely considered an element in the coup d'état that deposed Brazil's leftist President Joao Goulart in 1964,"[17] which was warmly welcomed by the Kennedy liberals, installing a national security state complete with torture, repression, and profits for the foreign investor. The story was re-enacted in Chile a few years later. During the Allende regime, the U.S. continued to supply arms while doing its best to bring down the regime, and was rewarded with the Pinochet coup, which again it welcomed.

The Iranian operations conform to a familiar pattern of policy planning, which is quite understandable and sometimes realistic. One can understand easily why it was publicly endorsed by Richard Helms and others in 1982.

The nature of U.S.-Iran relations under the Shah must also be recalled, in this connection. Iran was assigned a central role in controlling the Middle East under the Nixon doctrine, which was based on the recognition that the U.S. no longer had the capacity to enforce its will everywhere and must therefore rely on local "cops on the beat" (as Defense Secretary Melvin Laird put it), local proxies that would carry out their "regional responsibilities" within the "overall framework of order" maintained by the United States, in Henry Kissinger's phrase at the time.

A (partially tacit) tripartite alliance was constructed linking Iran, Saudi Arabia, and Israel under the U.S. aegis, committed to "defending" U.S. domination of the world's major energy reserves and protecting them from the primary enemy, the indigenous population, which might be infected with the "radical" idea that they should have a share in controlling U.S. resources which happen to be on their lands. This is, incidentally, only one example of a worldwide pattern.[18]

It is in this context that the "special relationship" with Israel developed as well. In 1958, the National Security Council noted that a "logical corollary" of opposition to radical Arab nationalism (in the technical sense of the term) "would be to support Israel as the only strong pro-West power left in the Near East." According to David Ben-Gurion's biographer, Michael Bar-Zohar, at that time Israel concluded a "periphery pact," which was "long-lasting," with Iran, Turkey, and Ethiopia, encouraged by U.S. Secretary of State John Foster Dulles. Through the 1960s, U.S. intelligence regarded Israel as a barrier to "radical nationalist" pressures against Saudi Arabia, and the conception of Israel as a "strategic asset" became institutionalised in U.S. policy after the U.S.-backed Israeli victory in 1967, and particularly after Israel's moves to block Syrian support for Palestinians being massacred in Jordan in 1970 at a time when the U.S. was unable to intervene directly for domestic reasons. With the fall of the Shah, Israel's role as a "strategic asset" serving as a base for enforcing U.S. interests in the region was enhanced. Meanwhile, Israel increasingly provided subsidiary services to the U.S. in southern Africa, Asia, and Latin America. [19]

About 1970, a split developed among U.S. elites over U.S. policy in the region. This was symbolised by the controversy between Secretary of State William Rogers, who advanced a plan for a political settlement of the Arab-Israel conflict along the lines of the international consensus of the time, and Henry Kissinger, who argued that a "stalemate" must be maintained, his reason for backing Israel's rejection of Sadat's February 1971 offer of a full peace settlement along the general lines of official U.S. policy. Kissinger's views prevailed. Since that time his confrontationist hardline opposition to a genuine political settlement has dominated U.S. policy, which has preferred to see an Israeli "strategic asset" playing its role in U.S. control of the region by the threat or use of force.

This explains the continued U.S. commitment to block a political settlement, which would lead to Israel's integration into the region. The U.S. backed Israel's rejection of Sadat's 1971 proposal and his subsequent efforts, a stand that led directly to the October 1973 war, "Kissinger's war" as honest history would describe it. The same was true in January 1976, when the U.S. vetoed a U.N. Security Council resolution introduced by Syria, Egypt, and Jordan and backed by the PLO (actually "prepared" by the PLO, according to Israel's U.N. ambassador, Chaim Herzog), calling for a political settlement in accord with the international consensus, which by then included the concept of a Palestinian state in the occupied territories. There have been many similar occasions since.

The 1973 war convinced Kissinger and other U.S. planners that Egypt could not be simply dismissed. They therefore turned to an alternative plan: to exclude the major Arab deterrent force from the military conflict so that Israel would then be free, with increasing U.S. support, to integrate the occupied territories and attack its northern neighbour. These plans culminated in the Camp David agreements of 1978-79—that this was the essential meaning of Kissinger's shuttle diplomacy and Camp David was evident at the time and is now sometimes conceded in retrospect though usually regarded as "ironic"—and constitute the essence of what is called "the peace process" (another Orwellism) in the U.S. doctrinal system.

The U.S. has consistently sought to maintain the military confrontation and to ensure that Israel continues to be a "strategic asset." In this conception, Israel is to be highly militarised and technologically advanced, a pariah state with little in the way of an independent economy apart from arms production (often in coordination with the U.S.). It is to be utterly dependent on the United States and hence dependable, serving U.S. needs as a local "cop on the beat" and as a mercenary state employed for U.S. purposes elsewhere—for example, in support of near-genocide in Guatemala when domestic factors prevented the Carter and Reagan Administrations from participating as fully as they would have liked in this enterprise (though they did participate, contrary to many falsehoods). [20]

What about U.S. relations with the Arab world? First, the U.S. will act to ensure that it controls the major energy resources of the Arabian peninsula: this is a central principle of U.S. foreign policy, as it has been throughout the World War II period. It will therefore support "moderate nationalists," such as the ruling elites in Saudi Arabia, who are well known for their "moderation." Saudi Arabia, too, is called upon to enlist support for U.S. international terrorism, as already noted, and there should be little surprise at the revelation that it is deeply involved in the supply of arms to Iran along with its tacit Israeli ally and in U.S. terrorist activities in Central America, and probably elsewhere as well: southern Africa, for example.

At the same time, the United States will consistently oppose "radical nationalists" who stand in the way of its objectives. Libya is a typical example. While the U.S. appears to have supported Qaddafi's effort to raise oil prices in the early 1970s "in order to strengthen the position of the 'moderates,' such as Iran, Kuwait, and Saudi Arabia,"[21] Libya has increasingly been an obstacle to U.S. objectives, supporting Polisario (along with the United Nations) and anti-American elements in the Sudan, standing in the way of the U.S.-organised strategic consensus in North Africa, and so on.

Libya is officially declared to be a leading "terrorist state." That Qaddafi is a terrorist is clear enough; the latest Amnesty International report on political killings by governments, for example, observes that Libyan terrorism, which began at a serious level in the 1980s, has claimed no less than fourteen victims, mostly Libyans. No doubt more will be added; let us assume, to give U.S. propaganda the benefit of the doubt, that Amnesty International underestimated by a factor of, say, one hundred, a vast exaggeration as far as is known.

Even with these concessions to the U.S. doctrinal system, Libya is barely a bit player in the arena of international terrorism. Consider the single example of El Salvador, where, during the same years, the U.S. organised and supported state terrorism that claimed tens of thousands of lives—international terrorism, given the role of the mercenary army supplied, trained, organised, and directed by the U.S., with direct participation of the American air force when necessary. And this is only one case.

In the earliest days of the Reagan Administration, Libya was designated as a prime target for its campaign against "international terrorism." This campaign was taken very seriously by U.S. elite opinion—including the media—despite its manifest absurdity, as the U.S. openly and eagerly geared up for renewed international terrorism. This policy was concealed over the years with various Orwellian euphemisms such as "counterinsurgency," "low-intensity war," defense against "subversion," or "internal aggression" (Adlai Stevenson's inspired phrase, referring to U.S. international terrorism in South Vietnam in the early 1960s).

Repeated confrontations with Libya have been provoked or invented on the flimsiest of pretexts, generally for domestic purposes, such as gaining support for the intervention force aimed primarily at the Middle East (the Rapid Deployment

168

Force, now the Central Command, which also has its eyes on Nicaragua), support for the *contra* armies attacking Nicaragua, and in general to reinforce the mood of reactionary jingoism required to implement Reaganite policies.

In this connection, we should bear in mind that the Reagan Administration faced a rather serious problem from the outset. Contrary to many illusions, its major policies have quite generally been highly unpopular. The population continues to support social rather than military spending and to oppose the programme of enhancing state power and converting the state, more than ever, into a welfare state for the rich—one major function of the Pentagon system, which serves to provide a forced public subsidy to high-technology industry in the system of state-managed public subsidy, private profit, called "free enterprise." The public has also generally opposed the "activist" foreign policy of subversion, intervention, international terrorism and aggression hailed as "the Reagan doctrine."

There is a classic way to deal with the problem of bringing a reluctant population to accept policies to which it is opposed: induce fear, in accord with Mencken's dictum. Therefore, we must have confrontations with the Evil Empire bent on our destruction, "the monolithic and ruthless conspiracy" committed to thwart our global benevolence and to destroy us, in John F. Kennedy's phrase during a rather similar period of U.S. history.

But confrontations with the Evil Empire are dangerous. The solution is to create "proxies" of the Evil Empire, which can be attacked with impunity since they are weak and defenseless. Libya is perfect for the role, particularly against the background of rampant anti-Arab racism in the United States, and within the general context of the "campaign against international terrorism"—that "plague of the modern world" against which the terrorist commanders in Washington must defend Americans, according to various "Operation Truths" conducted by the ideological institutions. It is quite easy to kill many Libyans without cost—indeed with many cheers at home, including enlightened liberal opinion—as Americans defend themselves against the "evil scourge of terrorism."

One such example was the U.S. bombing of Tripoli and Benghazi, the major single episode of international terrorism in 1986. It was obvious at the time, but concealed by the media, that there was no credible evidence of Libyan involvement in the discothèque bombing in Berlin that served as the pretext for this bombing. It was the first bombing in history scheduled for prime-time television, that is, precisely for 7 p.m. EST, when the U.S. channels air their national news—pre-empted, of course, by this exciting display and then effectively controlled by the state propaganda system in the crucial early period, with media complicity. By now, it is tacitly admitted that evidence of Libyan involvement was meagre or nonexistent. It follows that the bombing of Libya, with some one hundred people killed, according to press reports, was sheer unprovoked international terrorism, though no respectable commentator will draw the obvious conclusion.

This act of violence succeeded. It aroused jingoist passions at home and helped prepare the ground for ramming through support for the *contras* a few months later along with other elements of the Reaganite programme. There was a negative response in Europe, apart from France, but that was absorbed. In effect, U.S. violence turned up the ratchet a notch; it raised the level of expectations as to what the "crazy Americans" might do next.

What do they intend to do next? One possibility is a direct invasion of Nicaragua in support of "democratic elements," as they will be called by the government and the media. Another likely scenario is that sooner or later Israel will attack Syria on some contrived pretext, much as in the case of the 1982 invasion of Lebanon. As long as the U.S.-backed military confrontation persists, Israel can hardly allow any Arab state or combination of states to approach it in military power, for fear of destruction. Many Israeli commentators regard a Syria-Israel war as inevitable with only the timing in doubt, and some (such as the highly-regarded military specialist Ze'ev Schiff) predict that it will turn into a regional war that might also lead to expulsion of the Palestinian population from Israeli-controlled areas.[22]

But Syria is a Soviet ally, and Israel cannot attack it without assurance that the U.S. will deter the USSR from supporting its ally. Such an attack, then, might be accompanied by U.S. bombing of Syria ("in defense against terrorism"). This would put the Soviet Union on notice that it must, as always, keep away and not inhibit U.S.-backed Israeli military operations. Such steps might lead to global war, but U.S. elites, particularly of the Reaganite variety, are likely to be willing to face that risk, as they have been in the past.

The next two years could be extremely dangerous. The Reaganites want to leave a permanent stamp on American politics, whatever the outcome of the next election. They want to prove that violence pays. They want to overcome "the sickly inhibitions against the use of military force," as Norman Podhoretz put it, mimicking Nazi intellectuals.

The propaganda system has constructed a series of demons: the Sandinistas, who are a "cancer" that must be destroyed (the rhetoric of George Shultz, Reagan's speech writers, and others); Qaddafi, the "mad dog of the Middle East"; Arafat, "the father of modern terrorism"; and Castro, who threatens to take over the Western hemisphere in the service of the USSR. If they can be destroyed by violence, the long-term effects on American culture will be profound. There will be no more "wimps" making treaties and entering into negotiations, no concern for political settlements, international law, and similar tommyrot. Rather, the political system will be dominated by violent thugs, who get their kicks out of sending their client military forces and goon squads to torture people who cannot fight back—what is called "conservatism" in contemporary Newspeak.

It may be that the recent scandals will impede such plans, or they might accelerate them, if the more desperate Reaganites feel that their opportunities will be lost. We may be heading into extremely hazardous times.

171

Notes

1. On the facts as leaked in England, see Alexander Cockburn, *The Nation*, Nov. 22, 1986. Some of those involved claim that they were not objecting to the contents of the article but only to the inappropriateness of allowing a discussion of "thought control" in a society that "is unusual if not unique in the lack of restraints on freedom of expression" (my opening words) in a journal devoted to censorship. That claim is untenable. The journal has published articles of this nature before without evoking a hysterical response, threats to cancel subscriptions, letters from the State Department, etc.; see, e.g., Carole and Paul Bass, "Censorship American-Style," dealing with how controversial stories are killed by "market forces and weak-kneed publishers" (*Index on Censorship*, March 1985). The difference is that in the present case, the article dealt with media treatment of Israel.

2. *America and the World 1983, Foreign Affairs*, Winter 1983.

3. *The Boston Globe*, Oct. 28, 1986; Nov. 4, 1986. Robert C. Johansen, "The Reagan Administration and the U.N.: The Costs of Unilateralism," *World Policy Journal*, Fall 1986.

4. Richard Bernstein, "The U.N. Versus the United States," *The New York Times Magazine*, Jan. 22, 1984.

5. Michael White, *The Manchester Guardian Weekly*, Nov. 9, 1986, reporting from Washington. This is not evidence that the world is being "Finlandised" or "taken over by Communists," as the U.S. extreme right wing fantasises; the same poll shows that the European population is very critical of the USSR.

6. K. Jeffrey Smith, *The Washington Post*, Nov. 9, 1986.

7. The plan was apparently activated in a secret National Security directive of Jan. 4, 1983 (No. 77, *Management of Public Diplomacy Relative to National Security*). Alfonso Chardy, "Secrets Leaked to Harm Nicaragua, Sources Say," *The Miami Herald*, Oct. 13, 1986.

8. *Newsweek*, Aug. 3, 1981. On the U.S. disinformation programme and the carefully-leaked plots to kill Qaddafi, conduct terrorism, etc., as well as the fabricated Libyan threats, see the bitterly anti-Qaddafi study by P. Edward Haley, *Qaddafi and the United States Since 1969* (Praeger, 1984). On other disinformation programmes and media cooperation, see my *Turning the Tide: The U.S. and Latin America* (Black Rose Books, 2nd revised

edition, 1987); Edward S. Herman and Frank Brodhead, *The Bulgarian Connection* (Sheridan Square, 1986).

9. Alfonso Chardy, Knight-Ridder Service, *The Boston Globe*, Oct. 28, 1986.

10. Robert Reinhold, "Ex-General Hints at Big Role as U.S. Champion of Contras," *The New York Times*, Oct. 14, 1986. Chris Horrie, *The New Statesman*, Oct. 31, 1986, reporting on the Annual Conference of the World Anti-Communist League, noting in particular the prominence of RENAMO (the South African-backed guerrillas terrorising Mozambique) and their cozy relations with Singlaub, and probably the U.S. Administration. Scott Anderson and John Lee Anderson, *Inside the League* (Dodd, Mead & Co., 1986); only the Anti-Defamation League and the U.S. government concealed documentation and refused to cooperate with their research, they report.

11. On these matters, see my *Turning the Tide. op. cit.*, and sources cited.

12. On these matters, see my *Fateful Triangle: Israel. the United States, and the Palestinians* (Black Rose Books, 1984), p. 457f.

13. Michael Widlanski, "The Israel/U.S.-Iran Connection,"*Austin American Statesman* (Tel Aviv), May 2, 1986.

14. See William C. Rempel and Dan Fisher, "Arms Sales Case Putting Focus on Israel's Policies," *The Los Angeles Times*, May 5, 1986, noting that "veteran American investigators" say that "Israel has long been regarded as a conduit for secret arms sales" and that "there is little question that the flow to Iran of Israeli arms, at least, has continued" during the past five years, citing a West German estimate of a half billion dollars of military equipment. Douglas Frantz, "Israel tied to Iranian arms plot," *The Chicago Tribune*, April 24, 1986; Reuven Padhatzur, *Ha'aretz*, April 28, 1986. Much material of this nature has been circulated by Jane Hunter, editor of the excellent journal *Israeli Foreign Affairs*.

15. Leslie H. Gelb, "Iran Said to Get Large-Scale Arms from Israel, Soviet and Europeans," *The New York Times*, March 8, 1982.

16. Patrick Seale, "Arms dealers cash in on Iran's despair," *The Observer* (London), May 4, 1986.

17. Miles Wolpin, *Military Aid and Counterrevolution in the Third World* (Lexington Books, 1972), pp. 8, 128, citing Congressional Hearings and, on Brazil, *The New York Times*, Nov. 1, 1970.

173

18. For further discussion, see my *Towards a New Cold War* (Pantheon, 1982); Laird, cited by Thomas Ferguson and Joel Rogers, *Right Turn* (Hill & Wang, 1986), p. 97, an important discussion of factors in domestic affairs briefly reviewed here.

19. For more on these matters, see my *Towards a New Cold War*, *op. cit.*, and *Fateful Triangle*, *op. cit.*

20. See my books cited earlier for documentation; also Allan Nairn, *The Progressive*, May, Sept., 1986.

21. Maley, *op. cit.*, p. 31.

22. See Ze'ev Schiff, "The Spectre of Civil War in Israel," *Middle East Journal*, Spring 1985.

WORK AND MADNESS
The Rise of Community Psychiatry

by Diana Ralph

In this meticulously researched and immensely readable book, Diana Ralph takes on the community mental health systems. In a penetrating analysis of the expansion and innovation of mental health practices since the second world war, she argues that these changes have not been simply quantitative but that a qualitative shift has taken place in the definition and treatment of so-called mental health disorders.

These changes cannot be explained by available social theories whether liberal, Marxist or the radical anti-psychiatry approaches. Ralph proposes an alternative "labour theory" which situates the ideological origins of contemporary psychiatric practices within the tradition of industrial psychology and the needs of industrial management for control and regulation of the work force.

Dr. Ralph teaches social work at the University of Regina. She has been involved in a range of progressive issues including trade union and unemployment issues, occupational and environmental health programmes, native people's rights, and women's issues. She has also worked in a large mental health hospital and at counselling and rehabilitation centres.

3981 boul. St-Laurent
Montréal, Québec
H2W 1Y5

Publication date: May 1983
Paperback ISBN: 0-919619-05-3 $12.95
Hardcover ISBN: 0-919619-07-x $22.95
BLACK ROSE BOOKS No. L75

FEMINISM IN CANADA

From Pressure to Politics

edited by
Angela Miles & Geraldine Finn

This collection brings together for the first time the works of Canada's leading feminist scholars. From their different backgrounds in psychology, philosophy, sociology, economics, social work, and the literary arts, the contributors launch a swingeing attack on scientific orthodoxy in research practices and the androcentric biases in Western social thought.

After over a decade and a half of uneasy compromise, women's participation in "male stream" institutions has only served to exaggerate their sense of alienation and the futility of piecemeal reforms. Western institutions, their value systems and their research practices are antithetical to the fundamental concerns of women and do not allow for their articulation. In the world of male competition, pseudo-rationality and aggression, the qualities of caring, trust, emotionality and cooperation are either devalued or ignored.

If feminists are to have any real impact on the world, the rules of the game must be changed. Female values must be prioritized and must become the base line in feminist research and in the wider women's movement.

This is a scholarly book which reaches beyond the academic walls and which seeks an integration of thought and experience, research and politics.

Contributors: Margaret Benston, Marjorie Cohen, Yolande Cohen, Geraldine Finn, Madeleine Gagnon, Patricia Hughes, Helen Levine, Jill McCalla Vickers, Angela Miles, Mary O'Brien, Ruth Pierson, Alison Prentice, Jeri Dawn Wine, Carole Yawney.

315 pages
Paperback ISBN 0-919619-02-9 $12.95
Hardcover ISBN 0-919619-00-2 $20.95
BLACK ROSE BOOKS No. L74

2ND REVISED EDITION

TURNING THE TIDE

The U.S. and Latin America
by Noam Chomsky

Regarding U.S. policy in Latin America, *Turning the Tide* succinctly provides the most cogent available descriptions of what is going on, and why. It will be a central tool for everyone who wants to promote peace and justice in the Americas.

Noam Chomsky reveals the aim and impact of U.S. policy in Latin America by examining the historical record and current events. With this as backdrop, he also shows the connection between Latin American policy and broader nuclear and international politics and explains the logic and role of the Cold War for both super-powers. Finally, Chomsky looks at why we accept Reaganesque rhetoric in light of the role of the media and the intelligentsia in the numbing of our awareness. He concludes by describing what we can do to resist.

Turning the Tide is a succinct volume ideal for understanding the broad factors governing U.S. policy in Latin America, the role of the Cold War, and the role of the media and intellectuals with respect to each.

Noam Chomsky is professor of Linguistics and Philosophy and Institute Professor at M.I.T.; recipient of honorary degrees from the University of London, University of Chicago, Delhi University, and four other colleges and universities; fellow of the American Academy of Arts and Sciences, member of the National Academy of Arts and Sciences, and member of the National Academy of Sciences; author of numerous books and articles on linguistics, philosophy, intellectual history and contemporary issues.

Paperback ISBN: 0-920057-78-0   **$14.95**
Hardcover ISBN: 0-920057-76-4   **$29.95**

The Modern State

An Anarchist Analysis
by Frank Harrison

This important new contribution to theories of the State by political science professor and Bakunin scholar Frank Harrison provides a welcome departure from the straitjacket of orthodox and Marxist approaches.

Starting from the assumption that the theory and practice of State control thus far in history has operated to diminish the freedom of the individual and local groups, Harrison attempts a major reexamination of the history and theories of social change.

The disputes within the First International and the implications of their outcome are related to the historical trajectory of events surrounding the Russian Revolution, the Makhonist movement and the Kronstadt uprising as well as the recent Polish experience.

Harrison unearths some fascinating original material from the Russian Archives, including the writings and first-hand accounts of little known but important participants in the revolution.

Most of all, this book offers a fresh, much sought after perspective on important historical events, the theories behind them, and where research has to go if a truly liberatory perspective on social control is to be developed.

"...a useful guide to alternatives to the obsession with the all-powerful state in the nuclear age".

Canadian Journal of Political Sciences

227 pages
Paperback ISBN: 0-920057-00-4   **$12.95**
Hardcover ISBN: 0-920057-01-2   **$22.95**
Politics/Philosophy

THE COMING OF
WORLD WAR THREE

Volume 1

From Protest to Resistance
/ the International War System

Dimitrios I. Roussopoulos

This book is <u>not</u> about the arms race,
it is about the peace movement. In presenting
an analysis of the strengths and weaknesses
of actions for peace,
Dimitrios Roussopoulos shows us what
we must really do to prevent a third world war.

ISBN: 0-920057-02-0 $14.95

BLACK ROSE BOOKS

Write for free catalogue of more than 110 books:

Black Rose Books
3981, boul. St. Laurent
Montréal, Québec
H2W 1Y5

Printed by
the workers of
Ateliers Graphiques Marc Veilleux Inc.
Cap-Saint-Ignace, Qué.
for
Black Rose Books Ltd.

69
9459 4

9592 6